Praise for *The Year Without Pants*

"*The Year Without Pants* is one the most original and important books about what work is really like, and what it takes to do it well, that has ever been written."

— **Robert Sutton**, professor, Stanford University, and author, *New York Times* bestsellers *The No Asshole Rule* and *Good Boss, Bad Boss*

"The underlying concept—an 'expert' putting himself on the line as an employee—is just fantastic. And then the book gets better from there! I wish I had the balls to do this."

— **Guy Kawasaki**, author, *APE: Author, Publisher, Entrepreneur*, and former chief evangelist, Apple

"If you want to think differently about entrepreneurship, management, or life in general, read this book."

— **Tim Ferriss**, author, *New York Times* bestseller *The 4-Hour Workweek*

"With humor and heart, Scott has written a letter from the future about a new kind of workplace that wasn't possible before the Internet. His insights will make you laugh, think, and ask all the right questions about your own company's culture."

— **Gina Trapani**, founding editor, Lifehacker

"The future of work is distributed. Automattic wrote the script. Time for rest of us to read it."

— **Om Malik**, founder, GigaOM

"Some say the world of work is changing, but they're wrong. The world has already changed! Read *The Year Without Pants* to catch up."

— **Chris Guillebeau**, author, *New York Times* bestseller *The $100 Startup*

"You'll be surprised, shocked, delighted, thrilled, and inspired by how Word Press.com gets work done. I was!"

— **Joe Belfiore**, corporate vice president, Microsoft

"Most talk of the future of work is just speculation, but Berkun has actually worked there. *The Year Without Pants* is a brilliant, honest, and funny insider's story of life at a great company."

— **Eric Ries**, author, *New York Times* bestseller *The Lean Startup*

"WordPress.com has discovered a better way to work, and *The Year Without Pants* allows the reader to learn from the organization's fun and entertaining story."

—**Tony Hsieh**, author, *New York Times* bestseller *Delivering Happiness*, and CEO, Zappos.com, Inc.

"*The Year Without Pants* is a highly unusual business book, full of ideas and lessons for a business of any size, but a truly insightful and entertaining read as well. Scott Berkun's willingness to take us behind the scenes of WordPress.com uncovers some of the tenets of a great company: transparency, teamwork, hard work, talent, and fun, to name a few. We hear about new ways of working and startups, but we rarely get to see up close the magic that can occur when we truly tend, day in and day out, to building something bigger than ourselves."

—**Charlene Li**, author, *Open Leadership*, and founder, Altimeter Group

"Berkun offers a fascinating inside view of an unusual company that is experimenting with new ways of working. Some of it sounds crazy, but what geeks do today, the rest of us often end up doing tomorrow. It's a great story, packed with insights about corporate culture. Once you've seen how WordPress does things, you'll find yourself asking why your company works the way it does."

—**Tom Standage**, editor, *The Economist*

"Berkun balances keen observation, insights, and humor in this first-person account of a very 21st century organization. You'll be challenged to rethink your assumptions about how work is done, and work itself."

—**Eden Fisher**, executive director, Innovation Management Program, Carnegie Mellon University

"A wild behind-the-scenes ride inside one of the most successful and progressive companies on the planet. A timely and prescient view of the future of work."

—**Douglas Pyle**, vice president, JPMorgan Chase

"A personal and deeply insightful account of a new way of working in the connected world. Berkun has written an entertaining and thought-provoking read once again!"

—**Paolo Malabuyo**, vice president, Mercedes-Benz

"Berkun smashes the stereotypes and teaches a course on happiness, team culture, and innovation."

—**Alla Gringaus**, web technology fellow, Time, Inc.

THE YEAR WITHOUT PANTS

WORDPRESS.COM
and the future of work

SCOTT BERKUN

JB JOSSEY-BASS™

A Wiley Brand

Jacket design by Adrian Morgan
Cover art by Zachary Rathore/Getty (RF)

Published by Jossey-Bass
A Wiley Brand
One Montgomery Street, Suite 1200, San Francisco, CA
94104-4594—www.josseybass.com

Jossey-Bass books and products are available through most bookstores. To contact Jossey-
Bass directly call our Customer Care Department within the U.S. at 800-956-7739, outside
the U.S. at 317-572-3986, or fax 317-572-4002.

Wiley publishes in a variety of print and electronic formats and by print-on-demand. Some
material included with standard print versions of this book may not be included in e-books
or in print-on-demand. If this book refers to media such as a CD or DVD that is not
included in the version you purchased, you may download this material at http://
booksupport.wiley.com. For more information about Wiley products, visit www.wiley.com.

Library of Congress Cataloging-in-Publication Data
Berkun, Scott.
  The year without pants : WordPress.com and the future of
work / Scott Berkun.—First edition.
  pages cm
  Includes bibliographical references and index.
  ISBN 978-1-118-66063-8 (hardback); ISBN 978-1-118-72890-1 (ePDF)
ISBN 978-1-118-72895-6 (ePub)
  1. WordPress (Electronic resource) 2. Blogs—Computer programs. 3. Web
sites—Authoring programs. 4. Web site development. 5. Work environment. I. Title.
  TK5105.8885.W66
  338.7′61006752—dc23

2013027687

Printed in the United States of America
FIRST EDITION
HB Printing 10 9 8 7 6 5 4 3 2

CONTENTS

THE YEAR
WITHOUT
PANTS

WHAT YOU NEED TO KNOW

Giving advice is easy; it's the listening that's hard. Authors are the worst at remembering this.

Many people wonder what would happen if a famous expert returned to the front lines. Would this person really practice what he or she had preached from the safety of books and lectures? Over the past decade, I've written four popular books, and I've wondered how much of this trap I'd fallen into myself. If I were a manager again, would I follow my own advice? I wanted to know. The question was when and where.

When Matt Mullenweg, the founder of WordPress, asked me to join his company, Automattic, and manage a team, it was a perfect opportunity. WordPress powers almost 20 percent of the websites in the world, including half of the top one hundred blogs on the planet. WordPress.com, where I'd work, was among the top fifteen most trafficked websites. Its success aside, its culture was unconventional. Employees were young and independent, and they worked from wherever in the world they wished. They rarely used e-mail, launched new work into the world every day, and had an open vacation policy. If a work culture qualified as being from the future, this was it. I told him I'd do it if I could write a book about my experience. He said yes, and here we are.

This book has two ambitions: first, to share what I learned as an old dog in a futuristic workplace and, second, to capture the behind-the-scenes story of a good team at a fascinating company. I'll share what I learned, what I loved, and what drove me crazy, with insights for the rest of the working world.

The book is roughly chronological and based on my journal. The fancy term for this approach is *participatory journalism*, which means the writer, in this case me, doesn't merely report from the safety of the sidelines but reports from being in the middle of things. The advantage is intimacy. I'm honest in ways most books are not. The disadvantage is perspective: my story takes center stage even if other people's efforts were more important, which they often were. To balance the story, some chapters take a much wider view than my own tale.

WordPress and Automattic have noble ambitions, and I wish them the best. The candor of what follows honors the work they do and their willingness to share so others can learn.

CHAPTER 1

THE HOTEL ELECTRA

When Mike Adams wrote code, he put the back of his laptop on his legs and looked down at the screen. His fingers hung over the edge of his keyboard as if his wrists were broken. He looked like a happy astronaut writing in space, whimsically violating the rules of conventional physics. His brilliance reflected this independence as he regularly found his way through challenges with a grace matched by only a handful of engineers in the world. At twenty-nine years old, he was young enough not to have repetitive stress injuries to his body, but watching him work in comical contortions across various sofas and couches made it hard to believe this would last. Behind his thick glasses and fuzzy beard resided an iron will for solving problems. He often worked long hours immune to hunger or other physical discomforts until his understanding reached his level of satisfaction. His proficiency was all the more impressive because he'd never read a book on computer science. He was self-taught, brilliant, collaborative, and, at times, hysterically funny. And the best part is he worked on my team.

There were four of us hard at work in the lobby of the ominously named Hotel Electra in Athens, Greece. As is the case with many other famous Greek characters, Electra's tale is a delightful mix of revenge and matricide. According to Sophocles, she plotted with her brother to have her mother and stepfather killed to avenge the murder of her father. Just imagine how fun holiday dinner must have been at their house. Sophocles' tale is perhaps the inspiration for Shakespeare's *Hamlet*, but no one really knows. For me, whenever our work in Athens turned sour, I couldn't help but think of Elektra and all the things that go wrong with families and teams. I kept this to myself, of course: leaders should never joke about mutiny. Our team had been getting along well, and I didn't want anything, mythological or practical, to get in our way.

We were called Team Social, one of many teams of programmers working on a website called WordPress.com. This singular website is where millions of popular blogs and other websites live, and it's the fifteenth most trafficked website on earth. My team's job was simple: invent things to make blogging and reading blogs easier. If you watched us work in that hotel lobby, you'd have discovered many unorthodox and courageous methods in how we worked. Actually, that's not true. There are many unorthodox methods, but in watching us work, you'd be unlikely to notice them. With a superficial glance, you'd assume we weren't working at all.

We sat in a small lounge across from the hotel bar, tucked around a blind corner of the large lobby. It's as if the architect had been offered a bonus by the bartenders to make the bar hard to find, and he succeeded. We commandeered a set of puffy red chairs and couches, shaping them into a semicircle of web development, a veritable fortress of geekdom. The yellow walls behind us had small prints of late Renaissance family portrait paintings in thick wood frames. They were obscured by the glare from gold light fixtures, each tilting haplessly away from each other, a glare that made our laptops harder to see. The shared glass coffee table between us was too low, meant for coffee cups and bags of souvenirs rather than use as a makeshift desk for a team of engineers. To provision for power, we unplugged one of the floor lamps in the corner, an act, we believe, has made the sole bartender, a portly middle-aged Russian man, refuse to serve us despite our enthusiasm for overpriced, hand-delivered, umbrella-laden cocktails.

While I'm a decade older than the rest of the team, we all look to be in our mid- to late twenties. To any observer, it would seem we are simply spoiled young travelers choosing to play with our laptops and gadgets in a horror show of hotel discomfort and decor confusion rather than enjoying the glorious tourism opportunities Athens provides. Had we stood in the lobby carving ice sculptures with chainsaws, the work itself would provide a spectacle for observers. Hotel visitors passing through would have stopped and stared, asking questions, intently curious about what we were doing and how it was done.

But all of our work was invisible, hidden inside the glowing screens of our laptops. What no one could possibly know is at the click of a button from any of our web browsers, we could launch features that would instantly have an impact on millions of people around the world. Yet for anyone sitting nearby, for all they knew we were playing solitaire. An amazing thing about our digital age is that the person next to you at Starbucks might just be hacking into a Swiss bank or launching multiwarhead nuclear missiles continents away. Or maybe he's just on Facebook. You can't tell the difference unless you're nosy enough to peek over his shoulder.

Hidden behind our ordinary appearance were unusual facts. Although we were coworkers, our sitting together was a rare occurrence. Most of the time we worked entirely online. This meeting in Athens is only the second time we have all worked in the same room. We all met once before at Seaside, Florida, where the annual company meeting was held a few weeks prior. To convene at the Elektra, I'd flown in from Seattle. Mike Adams was from LA. Beau Lebens, who I'd bet moonlighted as a secret agent, was born in Australia but lived in San Francisco. Andy Peatling, a charmingly smart British programmer, split his time between Canada and Ireland.

The very idea of working remotely seems strange to most people until they consider how much time at traditional workplaces is spent working purely through computers. If 50 percent of your interaction with coworkers is online, perhaps through e-mail and web browsers, you're not far from what WordPress.com does. The difference is that work at WordPress.com is done primarily, often entirely, online. Some people work together for months without ever being on the same continent. Teams are allowed to travel to meet a few times a year to recharge the intangibles that technology can't capture, which explains our Athens trip. We specifically chose Greece because our boss suggested it, and we quickly said yes before he changed his mind. But the rest of the year we worked online from wherever in the world each of us happened to be.

Since location is irrelevant, Automattic, the company that runs WordPress.com, can hire the best talent in the world, wherever they are. This indifference to physical location is a fundamental assumption of how the company, founded in 2005, is organized and "managed." I put *managed* in quotes because, as I explain later, we are not managed at all in any conventional business sense. Initially the company was entirely flat, with all employees reporting directly to the company founder, Matt Mullenweg. In 2010 he and Toni Schneider, the CEO, decided things were too chaotic, even for them, and considered a better way: they split the company, which by that time had fifty employees, into ten teams.

Every team had one lead, the first hierarchy in company history. The lead role was loosely defined, and it was left to every team to figure it out for themselves. From Matt and Toni's perspective, running simultaneous experiments was a good thing. They could more quickly learn which things might work and which didn't. As an additional experiment, as if all this wasn't crazy enough, they picked one person from outside the company to be one of the leads. That person was me. This meet-up in Athens was historic for the company: it was the first time this new concept called a team had met together in what would be known as a team meet-up.

I'd only been at the company for ten weeks and didn't know my team well, but clearly they were talented. Mike Adams was the eighth employee at the company. He was on track for a PhD in quantum computing, a subject that I won't even try to explain, but his informal involvement with WordPress had grown into a passion. When Matt offered him a job, he left quantum computing behind and has thrived ever since. Beau Lebens, the most versatile programmer on the team, had worked at other companies, experience most coworkers at WordPress.com didn't have. His range of abilities beyond programming, from Krav Maga (the Israeli self-defense technique) to survival training, explains why he'd be near the top of my list for people to share a foxhole with. Despite his many talents, he seemed good-natured, humble, and cool-headed. Andy Peatling complemented the team perfectly: he excelled at the kinds of programming that Beau and Mike didn't, mainly the user-facing parts of software. He was fast at trying new things out, a skill all creative teams need. The three of them together formed a young, strong, confident team, regardless of who led them.

From Mullenweg's brilliant, or possibly mad, perspective, what made me interesting for the job was my experience leading teams, combined with my complete inexperience working anywhere like WordPress.com. Whereas the culture of WordPress.com, a company of sixty people at the time, was highly autonomous and rooted in open source culture, I'd spent my career at Microsoft and consulting with other large Fortune 500 organizations. The very idea of teams was a dramatic change for the company but not for me. There was genius here: match people together who must depend on each other to survive, only for different reasons. Mullenweg believed I could exemplify how teams should function, and the company could teach me a different way to think and work.

But we also agreed there were no guarantees: my hiring could be a disaster. What if the differences were too great? What if I failed to be productive remotely? Or the culture at WordPress.com rejected the entire idea of leads and teams? There were many big questions. But I confess the uncertainty was central to why I wanted the job. Whatever happened, there'd be a good story to tell, and that story starts with my first day.

CHAPTER 2

THE FIRST DAY

I was hired as employee #58 at Automattic in August 2010, three months before my team would visit Athens. There are no formal interviews for positions at the company. No one asks trick questions like why manhole covers are round or how many Ping-Pong balls fit on a 747 airplane.[1] Instead they hire by trial. This means you are asked to do a simple project. You get access to real tools and work on real things. If you do well, you're offered a job. If you don't, you're not. The many phony parts of hiring, from inflated résumés to trying to say what you think the other party wants to hear, disappear. Rather than fumbling in abstractions, you prove your ability through doing tasks you'd do in the job. It's simple and brilliant. Since all work can be done remotely, candidates don't have to fly anywhere. They can do their trial work from wherever they are. Some candidates can't find time to do the trial project; they are the ones who fade away in the running in favor of those who can.

My hiring was unique. There was no simple trial project for a leader, in part because leads didn't yet exist at the company. The company was entirely flat, with everyone reporting to Mullenweg. Instead of a giving me a trial, Mullenweg had read my books and invited me to consult with Automattic twice over the years. One of my recommendations was to move from a flat organization to a team structure. This was an obvious solution to a major frustration among employees: how centered things were on Matt and how they wanted to take on bigger projects than they could alone. But the challenge was that the culture strongly resisted hierarchy. Employees were fiercely independent and resisted anything that smelled like corporate culture. For many of them, the company was the largest they'd ever worked at. The idea of teams and lead roles was loaded with uncertainty. And I had my own challenge: by joining the company, I'd be an instrument of my own advice. If the change to teams failed, I'd have two reasons to be blamed. I never imagined when I offered the advice that I'd play a role in making it happen.

In the weeks before my first day, I was told my first meeting would be at 10:00 a.m. on Monday, August 4, so I had plenty of time to mull over the challenges I might face. I was an old school guy, and this was a new school company. What if I was out of touch? My best leadership tricks depended on being in the same room with people. Not being able to look folks in the eye in tough situations feels wrong. Would you propose marriage to someone online? Or tell a child her mother was dead in a text message? I worried that what made me good at work wouldn't transfer to a completely online environment. And I also had the usual assortment of ridiculous imaginary concerns. For example, I considered the possibility that Automattic made a mistake with the paperwork and didn't really mean to hire me; they meant to hire Flott Flerkun. Or perhaps there was an evil secret, like that everyone only spoke French and had Tourette's syndrome, or that my coworkers were inmates at Sing Sing Prison doing life sentences for murdering writers. It's a big and sometimes cruel universe, and working with people you haven't met is a roll of the dice.

Worries aside, on August 4, I rose from bed with only a few minutes to spare. At 10:00 a.m., I was supposed to meet with Hanni Ross, one of the team managers at WordPress.com. I had plenty of time since my commute was barely fifteen seconds. If it wasn't for my rotweiller-labrador Griz blocking my way in the hall, teasing me with his enormous rope toy, I could have done it in ten seconds. Griz followed me to my desk in my office and laid down at my feet.

I told him I had a new job, but he didn't believe it. It was all the same to him. This is one big problem with working remotely: no one believes you have a job at all. If they don't see you walk out the door, doubts linger.

I was told my first three days would be spent in training, but the surprise was that this wouldn't be training for the job I was hired for. Instead I'd be trained in customer support. All new employees work with the dedicated support team before starting their primary job. Working in support seemed to me an important but largely thankless job. Few people in the history of the world have called a support line simply to say, "Thanks for making a great product! You're awesome!" and then hung up the phone. Even for free products like WordPress, we are complaint-oriented creatures. Praise, however deserved, is harder to come by. I don't know of a single company that has a compliment reception department to match the one for complaints.

I worked in support once before when I was a student at Carnegie Mellon University. While the pursuit of support is admirable, I learned I was not well suited to the task. In my jaded estimation, people who contacted support were divided into two annoying piles. First are those with urgent and complex issues. If their problem wasn't urgent or complex, they'd find answers some other way. The second, and larger, pile are the lost and the lazy (L&L). Working in support demanded endless repetition because the lost and the lazy hit the same five basic issues again and again (coming in at #1 is, "How do I reset my password?"). I recall the moment I hit the existential crisis many in support hit of asking the universe, "Where are all the reasonable people?" and realized the answer was that many reasonable people don't contact support. They get answers from friends, coworkers, or by using the free documentation they find online. The saving grace was that I knew support at WordPress.com was e-mail only. I'd be free to make snarky faces at any ridiculous support requests I had to answer, and no one would know except Griz, who didn't care.

The staff at WordPress.com call support "Happiness." Therefore it's not the support team, but the *Happiness* team. And people who work in support aren't called tech support staff; they're called *Happiness Engineers* (HE). I was dubious about this. I'm doubtful of attempts to change reality simply by changing something's name. I could call Griz a wonder-dog-supergenius (WDSG), but that won't stop him from spending most days chewing bones and chasing squirrels. Changing a name doesn't change reality. But I withheld judgment. The wise engage all new things with an open mind. I wouldn't learn anything new if I judged them before getting my hands dirty, despite how much more fun judging things with clean hands can be. After a few days in support, my opinion changed indeed.

My hands-on training consisted of six half-day sessions with different happiness engineers. My training schedule was posted on one of the internal blogs. After Wednesday, when training ended, I'd be let loose on the world:

Mon 2nd Aug: 10:00 a.m.–1:00 p.m.: Hanni Ross

Mon 2nd Aug: 2:00 p.m.–5:00 p.m.: Ryan Markel

Tues 3rd Aug: 10:00 a.m.–1:00 p.m.: Andrew Spittle

Tues 3rd Aug: 2:00 p.m.–5:00 p.m.: Sheri Bigelow

Wed 4th Aug: 10:00 a.m.–1:00 p.m.: Zé Fontainhas

Wed 4th Aug: 2:00 p.m.–5:00 p.m.: Hew Sutton

When I worked at Microsoft during its 1990s glory days, employees could listen in on phone calls from customers in trouble. Many companies do this. You know those recorded messages you hear that say, "This phone call may be monitored for quality control"? There's a real reason they say that: others are listening. For a short time, it was mandatory at Microsoft to listen in at least once. Microsoft even provided a database for managers like me that listed which products, and which issues with which products, caused the most support calls.

These efforts were useful, but they were impersonal. Listening to someone else or reading a report doesn't put a fist in your gut the way being the person responsible for fixing the problem does. Making everyone work in support forces everyone to take customers seriously, which we should since they pay our salaries. Despite my distaste for it, the idea of making all employees participate in support, regardless of their distaste, was fantastic.

A little before 10:00, Hanni requested a chat in Skype. *Here we go*, I thought. After a decade of self-employment, I was now working for someone else again. Skype lets you talk through voice or by typing in a chat window. Typing in a chat window was wildly more popular than voice at Automattic, which seemed odd at the time. Shouldn't this company be on the cutting edge of everything? Why type when you can talk? More on that later.

Hanni Ross: Hi, Scott
Berkun: Hey—good morning
Ross: Welcome is I suppose the word of the day!:)

Berkun: Indeed.

Berkun: I'm in your hands, as it were.

Ross: This is all a bit hilariously backward:)

Berkun: How so?

Ross: Well, in terms of you already being somewhat familiar with how things work, knowing a fair few people and so on.

Ross: Backward in a good way!

Berkun: Ah, yes. Well, assume I know less than you think:) Honestly, I really don't know how anything specific works. And I definitely know little about how support works.

Ross: Aha:)

Ross: I have to confess something

Berkun: I like confessions

Ross: I may or may not have joined matt for sake and also then karaoke last night.

Ross: This may or may not be linked to me typing with one eye closed

Berkun: Hair of the dog. Sake for breakfast!

Ross: I'm also all good now that I have crackers and water

Berkun: Sounds like prison.

Berkun: Which is oddly the same as hangover recovery food.

Ross: Hm, I'd never considered the possible ramifications of that connection before.

Here's something that rarely happens on a first day on a new job: two minutes into my first meeting, and I was already immersed in Automattic culture. While Automatticians, the company nickname for its employees, don't see each other often, they are intensely social when together. These informal company gatherings happen as often as family reunions and feel like them too, except everyone likes each other. And knows how to code. I knew that Hanni, who was studying for her law degree while working for WordPress.com full time, lived in Paris or London. She must have been visiting San Francisco for a few days. There are other

Automatticians in San Francisco, including Beau Lebens, and odds are good they were there too.

The Matt she referred to as her partner in crimes of karaoke was Matt Mullenweg, the founder of WordPress and the founder of Automattic, the company that runs WordPress.com. He's one of those famous people who appear on various top lists: PC World's Top 50 People on the Web, Inc.com's 30 under 30, Business Week's 25 Most Influential People on the Web. I've known many in positions of power like his, and most spend their energy competing with the people higher than they are on those lists. It's quite dull really. There's a deep emptiness in the lives of our most powerful people. Their drive for power is an attempt to fill that void. They remind me of the businessman in *The Little Prince* by Antoine de Saint-Exupéry. In the book, the businessman has all the stars in the universe but no idea what they are good for: he just always wants more of them. Too many company founders are just collecting stars. Mullenweg is one of the few I've known who created something as powerful as WordPress yet remembers what the stars are for.

Hanni and I spent the morning setting me up on the various systems. It was all a fog, as to be expected. I just did what she said, and when the website in question did what she said it should do, we moved on. When it didn't, she took some time to get it sorted out. She also made sure I was set up on IRC, an ancient chat program I'd used in college that's still popular among programmers on open source projects. IRC was like the company's hallway. While Skype was more for one-on-one communication, IRC was where you went to talk to large groups, find help, or seek out people who wanted to socialize. And since there are people working from nearly every time zone in the world, there was always someone online to help with a problem or joke around with when you're working.

One of the accounts I needed to set up had a problem, so Hanni handed me off to Barry Abrahamson, the benevolent lord of all of WordPress.com's systems. If you imagine a secret underground bunker with endless rows of humming web servers and a lone genius conjuring spells to keep it all running, that's Barry. The only difference is there is no bunker. And no rows of servers, at least not in his presence. All the machinery used to power WordPress.com is housed in data centers around the United States, and Barry controls everything from his home in Texas. He's among the most important people in the company, since all the work everyone else does depends on the systems he manages so well. I'd met him once before at WordCamp San Francisco 2009. I had tagged along to a family reunion–type gathering and shared a ride with him back to the hotel. I plead the Fifth regarding what he said in this chat:

Barry: howdy
Scott Berkun: yay—the cavalry has arrived.
Barry: last time I saw you, you were falling over in an elevator
Barry: at the palomar
Scott Berkun: I deny everything
Barry: haha
Barry: ok, few housekeeping things

You can tell from my chats with Hanni and Barry that they were charming. And smart. And with only text, they conveyed personality and warmth. To work at a remote company demanded great communication skills, and everyone had them. It was one of the great initial delights. Every corporation has the same platitudes for the importance of clear communication yet utterly fails to practice it. There was little jargon at Automattic. No "deprioritized action items" or "catalyzing of cross functional objectives." People wrote plainly, without pretense and with great charm.

And as my first day went on, it was clear there were no set scripts. No forms to fill out. No checklists of boring things to do. Everything was informal but worked. I noticed it was Barry, not an automated form or an intern, who walked me through the tedium of account setup. He wanted every new employee to know who he was. Some of this was a side effect of how small the company was.

When there are only fifty employees, there is no management overhead. Everyone works directly on something. Regardless of the reason, it was refreshing to be cared for so directly by people in important positions.

One boring task I did discover was manually entering my coworkers into my Skype. There was no automatic way to add the dozens of employees as contacts. While waiting for Hanni or Barry to do something, I'd go to the list and manually add people. I asked if there was an automated way to do this, as you'd expect in a smart company like this one, but none existed.

As this went on, I was interrupted on Skype by Beau, the first of many entertaining Skype chats I'd have with him:

Beau Lebens: [Please add me to your contact]
Scott Berkun: [Scott Berkun has shared contact details with Beau Lebens]
Lebens: Beat you to it!
Berkun: you rat bastard
Lebens: i heard you were having too much fun adding people, so thought i'd turn the tables
Berkun: Nice to see your name:)
Berkun: So how hung over is Hanni?:) I'm assuming you're both at HQ?
Lebens: both here, yes; she's surprisingly chipper, considering
Lebens: although I thought she was going to vomit on me earlier
Berkun: that's a good sign—when you don't get vomited on before noon

My morning continued with many stops and starts, just like all first days. One advantage to working in Skype is freedom of attention. It's rare that the other person fully expects you to hang on every word he or she types. Everyone understands it's just a window on the screen and that you may be focusing on other things. As I waited, I read documentation about WordPress or skimmed internal blogs inside Automattic. After a break for lunch,

I was scheduled to work with Ryan for more training. Ryan lived in St. Louis and was a few hours ahead of me in Seattle:

Ryan Markel: Nicely punctual, sir.

Markel: So how was your morning training shift?

Berkun: Slow—Not Hanni's fault—but spent most of the day so far just getting accounts and whatnot working. No idea if that's typical or not.

Markel: Yeah, it's pretty normal.

Berkun: Oh—just a heads up. I need to be offline 3:30 to 4pm my time. I work from home and have to take Griz and Max out (or they'll eat me).

Markel: I was going to tell you that I'm going to take at least 15 to eat with my family at that time, so perfect.

Markel: OK, so you've worked through your account stuff and everything (should) be set up.

Markel: Have you covered the WordPress.com admin UI stuff yet?

Berkun: Nope.

Markel: That's a good place to start, then.

Markel: The first thing you might want to do is to fire up a test blog on WordPress.com you can use for part of this purpose.

Ryan mentions, in an offhand way, something he calls "admin UI stuff." Despite his nonchalance, what he was referring to was something quite amazing.

After getting the appropriate security access, a little toolbar appeared at the top of my browser window when I visited any blog that ran on WordPress.com's servers. This toolbar, available only because I was working in support, granted me godlike powers. I could change how any blog looked. I could add posts, edit them, or delete ones even if they'd already been published. The toolbar itself was small and filled with confusing menus and weird symbols. But as he taught me what each option did, alarms went off in my brain. Anything the user of any blog could do, I could do. I could also do things no user could, like add credits for upgrade purchases, shut down a blog by marking it as spam, and more. The more he showed me, the more fascinated I was. It was like the moment in a bad superhero movie where the evil genius finally reveals his magic device that controls all computers or banks around the world, fulfilling his plan for world domination. In a movie, you know nothing like that could exist, but here at WordPress.com it did, and I had access to it. I had assumed, without thinking about it consciously, that I'd get a childproof version to learn on with all the dangerous things turned off. Ryan assured me that wasn't the case.

This was a surprise. The fact that I was still alone at home, Griz at my side and not in an office surrounded by coworkers, amplified how strange it felt to suddenly have this much power. But as the training went on, I realized something similar exists at many corporations. We just rarely see behind the scenes. If you use Google, or Facebook, or have an online bank account, some of their employees have a similar tool to the one at WordPress.com. There's no other way for them to do their jobs. To fix our problems, they have to get in there somehow. It's logical, of course, but during my first day of training, I had irrational feelings of discomfort. Unlike asking me to fix their car, where they can see me go under the hood and watch every move I make, fixing someone's blog meant they didn't realize I was there.

CHAPTER 3

TICKETS FOR CATURDAY

Most of Tuesday and Wednesday, the balance of my training days, were focused on tickets. Tickets, tickets, and more tickets. These were not happy tickets like to a Yankees game or a round-trip flight to Paris. Instead these were tickets of pain. There were nearly 20 million blogs, or websites, running on WordPress.com. Each one was someone's representation of themselves on the web. From blogs about politics, to photography, to cooking, to business—every category, interest, and philosophy was represented. And each of them believed that what they published online was the most important thing in the world. Whenever any of these bloggers had a problem, they'd go to Wordpress.com/support and report their story of woe. Each report received a unique number and was henceforth called a ticket by employees—as in, "This is a tough ticket," or, "I've seen this ticket before," or, "How long have you been working on that same ticket, Scott?"

The database entry for every ticket would automatically record information about the user that the lucky happiness engineer might need to solve the problem—things like the customer user name, the name of the person's blog, and technical details for which server the blog lives on. But the greatest wild card of all in all the data, and the most precious piece of information for any happiness engineer hoping to solve any ticket, is the customer's own perception of what is wrong. And the gap between what people think is wrong and what is actually wrong can be quite far indeed.

In some cases, customers simply write: "My blog is broken," which is sad, of course, but also infinitely vague. No one wants a broken blog, but this message is useless in helping solve the problem. It's like calling 911 and saying, "Save me," again and again and again as if the problem is in the person on the other line not realizing you need to be saved. That's never the problem, as the person on the other end saves people all day long. That's the entire job: waiting for people who need to be saved to call.

There is a lazy imagination that takes over when we're in a crisis. We behave as if the universe has shifted and shrunk down, placing our problem in the center of everyone's lives. And if that weren't enough, we assume omnipotence in the people we believe can help us—that somehow they know everything about us and what we were trying to do, as well as how to instantly fix it. Altogether it's tickets like these that are extra sad because their lack of detail guarantees there will be no immediate relief. Their panic ensures that the first response to the ticket will be a salvo of questions asking for more information. Instead of a life preserver, it's an interrogation. It's disappointing for everyone involved.

Months before I started at Automattic, some of the happiness engineers studied the kinds of requests that came in and realized that if they changed the user interface, they might get better information straightaway from customers. They decided to force customers to answer three good questions:

- What did you do?
- What did you see?
- What did you expect?

These are clever queries. They're often the first questions anyone doing support or first aid might ask someone in trouble.

However, it didn't do enough for one user, who left me a ticket with these answers:

> I did: Errors
>
> I saw: Errors
>
> I expected: Solutions.

I gave him a point for accuracy. Yes, he should expect solutions. But this sort of smarty-pants answering only slowed the process of giving this person happiness.

Another ticket I'd see later in my tour answered only, "Help!" to all three questions. Most tickets were more verbose, but they all revealed an outside-in view of how WordPress works. Much like a doctor has to translate a layperson's description of what's wrong into medical knowledge of how the body works, even good descriptions of problems required making a mental model of what the user was trying to describe and then mapping that model onto how I knew WordPress actually worked. Half the battle is the ability to translate, not just knowledge of how to fix things. Knowing how to fix things doesn't help if you can't figure out what's wrong.

In this sense, the training I received was perfect. It was indistinguishable from work. My trainers—Ryan, Andrew, Zé, Sheri, and Hew—picked tickets from the pile of unresolved issues and Skyped the link. I was expected to figure things out and find answers on my own, and they'd give hints when I got stuck. Many tickets were easy for anyone who used WordPress regularly. Others asked basic questions about features I'd never heard of but were still easily answered by reading the relevant documentation (written by other happiness engineers who'd answered the question before). But some were complex and required help. I'd ask my trainer, and he or she would point me in the right direction. In some cases I was told to go to IRC, the chat program all employees used, and ask for help there. I was apprehensive at first, but I discovered help was always available in just a few seconds, often offered by more than one person.

It was the community at work: people were willing to drop whatever they were doing to lend a hand to people they didn't know.

Most tickets demanded I look at the blog in my own browser to see what was going on. Each day I'd have firsthand exposure to the diverse things customers were doing. There were blogs about religion. Blogs about sports. People who loved great food and wanted to teach others how to make it. Every passion imaginable, and some unimaginable, moved through my hands. It felt like being a digital librarian chartered with tending to books on the shelves, keeping them in good order. Although I was being paid to do it and WordPress.com is a business, the fact that all the information in all of these blogs was free online to anyone in the world crossed my mind several times. We all suffer from bias in what we read, believing we see a wide range of ideas when in truth we filter on our politics and beliefs. But as I did my happiness tasks, I saw everything and felt good there was a way for so many people with different ideas to share.

When training ended, I was on my own to resolve tickets. After a few days, I had another chat with Matt. We'd chatted on Skype at least once a day, mostly me asking questions about my team and what I needed to know. During one of these conversations, Matt asked about my work in Happiness. I told him it was going fine. I asked him many questions about my teammates, the projects they were working on, and what his expectations were. He was polite and informative, but often he suggested I wait until after I was done with my support tour. I persisted. Maybe this tour requirement was soft, and I could skirt around it. Eventually I shook the tree enough to reveal a surprise: there were statistics for support tickets and I was underperforming:

[8/6/2010 10:56:57 AM]:

Matt: right now you should focus and do nothing but support, it's really important you excel there because so far you've been a bit slow so far and people informally look to support training stats as an indicator of future performance

Scott: ok—will do.

Scott: No one told me there was a scoreboard!

Matt: don't worry, your 14 tickets and 1 forum post are very cute

Scott: I didn't see Thurs mail from Beau or Andy—did u?

Matt: don't worry about it until you're done with support

Scott: Do you have an auto-responder yet for me that says "wait until your done with support?"

Matt: heh

The ticket statistics Matt informed me of were extensive. It showed for each employee tickets per day, week, month, or year. I had no idea there were statistics being recorded at all. You could view it various fancy ways: by hour, by date, by who had the most today or most for the week. It was a robust scoreboard for the entire company. Why wasn't this part of my training? Why didn't anyone refer to it once?

I returned to tickets with big questions on my mind. Was I supposed to have discovered this myself? How do I feel about being monitored? The last time I had a job where I was tracked by the number of widgets I did something with was . . . never. I filed manila envelopes into wall-sized file cabinets for a collections agency in Queens, but even they didn't track my performance this closely. As long as the huge stacks they'd give me each morning were gone by the evening, no one cared. There was plenty of visible feedback from my WordPress coworkers that my work was fine. But being alone with these numbers in my home office left me wondering if I was missing something. The sense of Big Brother and faceless competition was hard to shake. By the end of my first week, I had a total of forty tickets and answered one question on the public forums. The average happiness engineer did all that in an hour. This included my spending extra time on Caturday (a joking reference to the day generally called Saturday) motivated by Matt's chiding.[1] Even worse than being tracked was being tracked and being in last place.

| | Scott - WordPress.com | | | | Jun | Jul | Aug | Total |
| Stats for August 2010 | | | | 2010 | | | 363 | 363 |

Monday	Tuesday	Wednesday	Thursday	Friday	Caturday	Totals
Aug 2	Aug 3	Aug 4	Aug 5	Aug 6	Aug 7	
	2 tickets	7 tickets	1 tickets	17 tickets	13 tickets	40 tickets
	1 forums					1 forums
	0.3 hours					0.3 hours
Aug 9	Aug 10	Aug 11	Aug 12	Aug 13	Aug 14	
12 tickets	31 tickets	29 tickets	23 tickets	12 tickets		107 tickets
	4 forums	16 forums	30 forums	34 forums		84 forums
	9.7 hours			0.9 hours		10.6 hours
Aug 16	Aug 17	Aug 18	Aug 19	Aug 20	Aug 21	
33 tickets	30 tickets	30 tickets	8 tickets	4 tickets		105 tickets
	18 forums	2 forums	6 forums			26 forums
4.9 hours	1.9 hours					6.8 hours

Here's why famous experts who write books never go back to regular jobs: regular jobs are hard. Regular jobs mean you answer to others. Regular jobs mean you do regular, and often repetitive, things. Regular jobs mean you are not the center of attention and have to follow rules made by other people. Anyone who's an expert, guru, executive, or coach has likely lost any real sense of what real work is. We assume that because we can give advice on something, we are superior to those who take the advice, but that's not true.

Writing, for example, is certainly hard, and many people don't like to do it, but writers can start and stop whenever they want. There is no customer to argue with until the essay or book is finished. When faced with a troublesome paragraph, we're free to take a break or work on something else. But support is relentless. It's true I can work from any room in my home, or any coffee shop in the world, but the pressure isn't physical or local. Instead it's the knowledge more tickets are always waiting, demanding my attention. This pressure made me feel like a wimp for complaining about writing deadlines or tough lecture audiences. Those are comparatively simple stresses that I've come to know well and disarm. The psychology of support was foreign and intimidating.

The upside was that it forced me to learn. Every day I discovered new techniques and tricks, forced to learn them to answer hard tickets. Andrew and Hew recommended I take on at least one tough ticket a day because the goal for the tour wasn't just to survive or make some arbitrary quota but to learn. One hard ticket might take me hours to solve, but I'd learn entirely new areas of the product, which would help me down the line after the tour was over. Hanni also told me I'd break things as I learned, and this was expected. Learning to fix broken things was part of the job too.

But Matt's chiding confirmed there was a quota; it just wasn't stated anywhere. He implied that other employees look at other employees statistics and that's part of how they size them up. Was this true? How much was I being watched? There was no easy way to know. Liking competition and wanting to impress people, I committed myself to working as hard as could on my numbers, and over the next week my stats rose dramatically, hitting more than thirty tickets per day. But it didn't last long. Fatigue and frustration set in. Overall my results were disappointing: I never came close to the achievements of the happiness engineers.

It actually felt great, for the first week, when I helped someone. It was like unblocking a little stream so the happy little fish could swim on. Every closed ticket gave me the sense that things were a little more right in the world. But as weeks wore on, my resentment grew. Even with tickets that required ingenuity to figure out or to explain, it bothered me that only one person would benefit from my effort. And when that person succeeded because of my work, he or she would throw it away and never look at it again. There was no motivation for me to do great work, only good work. It was the opposite of why I wanted to be a writer. If I publish a great book, it can live on forever and be read by hundreds or thousands of people. There's good reason to make it as great as I can. But writing tickets was the opposite proposition of effort, and with each day, my morale declined. My literary ambitions made me arrogant about words and ill suited for high-volume writing.

Stats for August 2010

Anthony
1,810 tickets
0 forum posts
28 hours
14.3% of total

Andrew
1,240 tickets
27 forum posts
19 hours
10.0% of total

Naoko
1,162 tickets
38 forum posts
47 hours
9.5% of total

Hanni
886 tickets
24 forum posts
17 hours
7.2% of total

Mark
580 tickets
181 forum posts
7 hours
6.0% of total

Sheri
514 tickets
100 forum posts
39 hours
4.8% of total

Lance
281 tickets
327 forum posts
18 hours
4.8% of total

Ryan M.
423 tickets
75 forum posts
22 hours
3.9% of total

Michael Koenig
491 tickets
0 forum posts
0 hours
3.9% of total

Ran
460 tickets
0 forum posts
10 hours
3.6% of total

Hew
417 tickets
18 forum posts
41 hours
3.4% of total

Scott
252 tickets
111 forum posts
18 hours
2.9% of total

Nick
354 tickets
0 forum posts
1 hours
2.8% of total

Lloyd
311 tickets
0 forum posts
16 hours
2.5% of total

Ian
228 tickets
64 forum posts
9 hours
2.3% of total

Despite my best efforts, the support tour kicked my ass. On my last day I completed a paltry 4 tickets, ending with a total of 252 for the month. Anthony Bubel, a happiness engineer proudly working from Philadelphia, closed 1,810 tickets in roughly the same amount of time. I'd leave the tour demoralized but inspired. I was certain all organizations would improve if every new hire had to start on the front lines like I had. Unlike the graduates of the empty new-employee orientation events that companies inflict on recent hires, I could proudly say I'd simultaneously helped customers, improved my knowledge of the product, and befriended more than a dozen coworkers through actual work. But as good as I felt this was for me as an employee, I was thrilled to finally join my team and build something new.

CHAPTER 4

CULTURE ALWAYS WINS

Before my story continues, I need to tell you about how Word-Press started. This isn't simply because it's a great story, although it is, but to introduce its culture as a character in this book. While I won't bore you with grand theories of anthropology (I'll leave that to the professors), I'm certain that to learn from a place, you have to study how its culture functions. A great fallacy born from the failure to study culture is the assumption that you can take a practice from one culture and simply jam it into another and expect similar results. Much of what bad managers do is assume their job is simply to find new things to jam and new places to jam them into, without ever believing they need to understand how the system—the system of people known as culture—works. Much like the frustrated moron who slaps the side of a TV when it stops working, taking action without understanding the system rarely helps.

A favorite example of this tragic management habit is how in 1999 the famous design firm IDEO was featured on ABC's popular *Nightline* TV show. They demonstrated an idea development technique they used called a "deep dive" to redesign a shopping cart in just five days. Soon hundreds of companies were doing their own half-baked versions of deep dives, and, surprise, the results were disappointing. Somehow, despite how dedicated some were to following all the steps and all the rules, an element was missing, and they couldn't match the results they'd seen on the show. The missing ingredient was, of course, the primary one: the people involved. Watchers of *Nightline* worked at places with employees who were not as talented in design as IDEO's. But beyond their talent, IDEO employees shared values and attitudes that were not explicitly captured in the deep dive method despite how essential those things were for the method to work. In anthropology terms, this superficial mimicry is called a *cargo cult*, a reference to the misguided worship of abandoned airplane landing strips among tribes hoping for the goods that airplanes had delivered to return.

Every year new trends in work become popular in spite of their futility for most organizations that try them. These trends are often touted as revolutions and frequently are identified with a high-profile company of the day. Concepts like casual Fridays, brainstorming sessions, Lean, Six Sigma, Agile, matrixed organizations, or even 20 percent time (Google's policy of supporting pet projects) are management ideas that became popular in huge waves, heralded as silver bullets for workplaces. The promise of a trend is grand, but the result never is. Rarely do the consultants championing, and profiting from, these ideas disclose how superficial the results will be unless they're placed in a culture healthy enough to support them. No technique, no matter how good, can turn stupid coworkers into smart ones. And no method can magically make employees trust each other or their boss if they have good reason not to.

The best approach, perhaps the only approach, is an honest examination of culture. But culture is harder to understand than a meeting technique or a creativity method. And culture is scary because unlike techniques, which are all about logic, culture is based on emotion. Few people have the skills to evaluate, much less change, a culture, even if they have the courage to try. It's far safer to simply wait for the next trend to come along and rally behind it, hoping the excitement for the new method distracts everyone from noticing how little impact the previous method had.

In my story so far at WordPress.com, every employee I met was smart, funny, and helpful. They'd invested heavily in tools and systems but put the onus on employees, even new ones like me, to decide how, when, and where to do their work. These attributes of culture didn't arrive by some technique sprinkled around the company years after it started. How did it happen, then?

In 2002, eight years before I was hired and two years before Mark Zuckerberg would start Facebook, eighteen-year-old Matt Mullenweg, a recent graduate of Houston's High School for the Performing Arts, went to Washington, DC. An avid photographer, he wanted to add the pictures from his trip to his popular photo website, photomatt.net. He'd been using a program called Cafelog, but he was increasingly frustrated by it. He had recently learned that the main programmer behind it, Michel Valdrighi, had disappeared. Updates on the Cafelog website stopped and e-mails went unanswered. Mullenweg assumed the program was dead and he'd have to switch to something else, a painful choice. But something worried him more: he had ethical differences with the makers of all competing programs. They had restrictions for what users could do with the software, and that seemed wrong to Mullenweg.

While most software is copyrighted and closed, Cafelog had different rules. It did not have a copyright. Instead it had something called an open source license, or a copyleft. This meant anyone could copy the source code for Cafelog and do what they wanted with it, including making a competitor to Cafelog (that copy is known as a fork, as in a fork in the road). The wrinkle was that anyone who did this would have to use the same license in whatever they made—a little rule that had grand implications: it ensured that ideas inside software could live on and be useful in ways the original creator never imagined. The most popular copyleft license was something called a GPL, or general public license, and many open source projects used it, including Cafelog.

   This powerful idea inspired Mullenweg and gave him a choice. While he had majored in jazz saxophone in high school, he'd also learned to program. His father was an engineer and had encouraged Matt's interests in computers, leading to small projects that Matt did for friends and at school. But these were side projects, fixing issues with software other people had made. He thought maybe he had the skills to do something more ambitious and knew the only way to find out was to try. The copyleft license gave him the freedom to start from where Cafelog had left off.

   On January 23, 2003, in a post titled, "The Blogging Software Dilemma," he announced on his website he was going to start a new, unnamed project:

> My logging software hasn't been updated for months, and the main developer has disappeared, and I can only hope that he's okay.

> What to do? Well, Textpattern looks like everything I could ever want, but it doesn't look like it's going to be licensed under something politically I could agree with. Fortunately, b2/cafelog is GPL, which means that I could use the existing codebase to create a fork, integrating all the cool stuff that Michel would be working on right now if only he was around. The work would never be lost, as if I fell off the face of the planet a year from now, whatever code I made would be free to the world, and if someone else wanted to pick it up they could. I've

decided that this the [sic] course of action I'd like to go in, now all I need is a name. What should it do? Well, it would be nice to have the flexibility of MovableType, the parsing of TextPattern, the hackability of b2, and the ease of setup of Blogger. Someday, right?[1]

He wasn't sure what to expect. His website was popular, but how much that would help this effort was unclear. Regardless, he was committed. Since no one responded at first, it looked for certain as if he'd be working alone. His announcement post sat online for the whole world to see without receiving a single comment, not even to say good luck. On the web, even posts on popular blogs that don't receive attention in the first few hours never receive any at all.

But the next day another programmer who had used Cafelog, Mike Little, replied: "Matt, if you're serious about forking b2 [aka Cafelog] I would be interested in contributing. I'm sure there are one or two others in the community who would be too."

And that was it. No one else asked a question or cheered them on. Mike's comment would be the only one on the post for over a year. Like most other events that change the world, it didn't seem interesting to anyone except the people willing to do the work.

Since there were only two of them, each could work fast without annoying the other. Little worked from the UK, while Mullenweg stayed in Texas. Soon a friend of Matt's suggested the name WordPress, and when they released the first version a few weeks later, that's what it was called. By June 2003, with release .71, they'd made something that surpassed Cafelog and it quickly gained attention from stars in the tech world. A nice surprise was that Michel Valdrighi, the mysterious original developer of Cafelog, joined the project. His return both validated WordPress's momentum and suggested to other programmers that the people working on it were easy to work with. By August they had over ten thousand blogs using their software, with the number climbing every day.

It was one month later that my own history crossed with WordPress for the first time. In September 2003 I quit my job as a manager at Microsoft. It took me a year, my ninth there, to find the courage to leave. Like Mullenweg, I was at a crossroads but in a different direction. While he was just starting something, I was leaving something. I'd had a great career at Microsoft. I worked on the first five versions of Internet Explorer during the rise of the web. I learned from good managers and coworkers and was able to ship many diverse projects. But my fear was that if I stayed in the same place for a decade, I'd never leave. I wanted an interesting life, and as much as I didn't know what that meant, I was certain that working for the same company for ten years would not help me figure it out. I convinced myself my prospects would improve if I were unemployed. To be unemployed by choice meant I'd have no baggage and be free to learn a new way to be. My vague ambition was to write books, and off I went.

As I planned my exit during summer 2003, I looked for software to start a blog and get visibility for my writing online. Movable Type was the best known, but minutes into installing it, I hated it. The instructions were complex and easy to get wrong. Installing software is like a first date: if it can't be polite, smart, and generous, what should I expect later? I looked for something else and discovered WordPress. In five minutes, my blog was live. It was so easy I wondered if I'd missed a step, thinking of my experience with Movable Type.

On September 21 2003, the first day of my freedom and the birth of my writing career, I posted for the first time to my blog, using WordPress .71:

> Today was my last day at Microsoft. Several months (years?) of thinking about doing other things have ended. I am now unemployed. Handed in my badge and left building A. I stood outside for a good ten minutes looking at the building, laughing about how I couldn't get back in even if I wanted to.
>
> I have a few months to figure out what's next. I'm proud of myself for doing something that scared the crap out of me.[2]

WordPress did what good tools do: It stayed out of my way.[3] It was simple and fast and did what I needed, a design ethos I liked. The fact that WordPress was open source meant little to me. I liked the idea of open source, but I didn't care enough for it to drive my decisions. I'd used open source software before when studying computer science in college, including countless caffeinated hours writing code in EMACS, a brilliant editing program made by Richard Stallman (who coined the term *copyleft*). I used other tools that were open, or free, or in the public domain, but that was rarely the reason I chose them.

But for Mullenweg, open source was a central principle. He also cared how that principle attracted people with similar values. Programmers volunteered to write code for WordPress primarily because of the open philosophy work style he'd chosen. Every discussion WordPress contributors had was public: every discussion, decision, bug fix, and feature idea was listed out in the open. Anyone who was considering helping could easily see what Matt, Mike, and other developers were like to work with. Were they reasonable and friendly, or hostile and guarded? By reading a few web pages, anyone could easily find out. This transparency planted an important seed in the culture. People behaved knowing that their actions would be visible to future contributors. And since there would be no face-to-face meetings, how well you expressed yourself in words was critical to earning a good reputation.

By August 2003, WordPress's popularity and the number of volunteer contributors climbed rapidly and continued over the next five years. By 2007 it was one of the most popular software products online. Mullenweg was heralded as a visionary, named one of the most influential people in the world by *BusinessWeek* and *Time* magazines. It was amazing to watch but especially profound for Mullenweg, who never expected this to happen, much less while he was so young. And it wasn't the numbers or the potential for wealth that excited him. He saw thousands of different ways people were expressing themselves online—sharing stories, lessons, photos, and more, through the publishing tools WordPress provided for free. He wanted to ensure publishing was democratic for everyone—not just this year or next but forever.

The culture of WordPress grew practically, one decision at a time. He and other contributors made many decisions based primarily on what was best for the project, but eventually a philosophy emerged. I interviewed Mullenweg and other contributors to distill that philosophy down to three elements:

- *Transparency*. Since all discussions, decisions, and internal debates in the WordPress community are public, little is hidden. The spirit is that if you weren't willing to say something in front of your community, how much conviction could you have in it anyway?
- *Meritocracy*. Those who put in more time and made better contributions received respect. Authority was earned, not granted. There were few job titles or designations. People who merely complained were given less respect than people who made or fixed things.[4]
- *Longevity*. That WordPress was born from a failed project never left Mullenweg's mind. He wanted to ensure the project lived on forever. The open source license meant that even if Matt became evil-Matt and tried and tried to destroy WordPress, someone could fork the project and continue. Unlike contributions to a closed project, contributions to WordPress would be eternal.

None of these attitudes were forced into place. These ideals, which are characteristic of how Matt and Mike wanted to work, evolved into habits across the WordPress community. Looking at the size of the community today, it might seem there must have been magical powers used for people to work for free and follow these precepts. Was it Mullenweg's charisma? Did people expect to find jobs by contributing? There is no simple answer. The culture grew out of a small seed, just as all cultures do. And no singular decision defines a culture. Instead it emerges from a back-and-forth between a leader and the contributors, reinforcing some things and pushing others away. Mike Little and Mullenweg's collective attitude about working together was what influenced the first contributors who followed. When each new person joined, he or she tried to fit in, reinforcing it. Those who didn't like the culture left. By the time WordPress was popular, the community had jelled around these values even if they didn't notice them or know why they were there.

Often founders don't fully understand the seeds they've planted until much later. Talent is hard to find, especially at new organizations, which allows leaders to justify rushing to hire people who are selfish, arrogant, or combative. This is poison for culture, assuming you want a culture of generous, confident collaborators. Starting a company, or even a project team, is an exceedingly hard challenge, but in the scramble to survive, founders often hire to solve immediate needs and simultaneously create long-term problems. This mistake is common enough that Bob Sutton wrote a book, *The No-Asshole Rule*, to help executives recognize the damage these hires cause to culture.[5] No matter how many golden lectures a leader gives imploring people to "Be collaborative" or "Work as a team," if the people hired have destructive habits, the lecture will lose. And of course if the leader is the asshole, there is no hope at all. In the open source world, a disgruntled volunteer could always decide to fork the project and take it in his or her own direction, an escape valve from misery that corporations never provide.

For a brief time Mullenweg worked at CNET.com, but this lasted less than a year. During that time, competition with Movable Type became intense and hostile. His time at CNET helped him realize the limits of what the WordPress community could do on its own. Although WordPress was free, users needed a server to put it on, which they'd have to find on their own. He decided that to ensure a strong future for WordPress, he needed a small company, with a handful of programmers working full time, to go after these projects. In August 2005 he asked three well-known volunteer programmers from the WordPress community—Donncha O'Caoimh, Andy Skelton, and Ryan Boren—to quit their jobs and join Mullenweg's bootstrapped new company. He was completely honest: he told them there was no venture capital firm behind them and fully admitted that at age twenty-one, he had no experience doing any of what he was about to do. He also reminded them that the core philosophy of this corporation would be open source, which made it all sound even crazier, as it would mean they'd use a GPL license on all the code for everything they made. They said yes, and work began.

That company was called Automattic, a play on the word *automatic* but misspelling it intentionally to include Matt's name. Their first product was Akismet, a spam protection plug-in for WordPress. It was followed months later with WordPress.com, where anyone, anywhere on earth, could use WordPress completely for free, hosting included. And whenever the WordPress volunteer community released a new version, it would be automatically updated on WordPress.com. On November 2005, WordPress.com launched. Within a few weeks, 100,000 blogs were already using the new service. This was fantastic news for Automattic but troubling to some in the WordPress community. They feared that the existence of a corporation, and a private service like WordPress.com, conflicted with the open values of WordPress. Depending on what Automattic did, the playing field for themes, plug-ins, and other services related to WordPress might become slanted in its own favor. This tension remains for some of the hundreds of independent web and theme development companies that have chosen to depend on WordPress to make a living.

By the following year, Automattic had eighteen employees, many of whom Mullenweg had never met in person. He handpicked them out of the WordPress community, having worked with them entirely online. The company made enough revenue from Akismet to cover expenses but also secured $1.1 million in November 2005 from Blacksmith and Polaris (they'd do a second round with Polaris and True Ventures in 2008 for $29.5 million).[6] Later that month, Toni Schneider, whom Mullenweg had met for a long lunch in San Francisco, joined as CEO of Automattic. Schneider, a former executive at Yahoo, had founded and led several successful start-ups including Oddpost (a webmail service acquired by Yahoo) and Sphere (later acquired by AOL). This made him an excellent partner for Mullenweg who had little experience with managing a company.

Schneider had specific ideas about how to make a great company culture, ideas that Mullenweg shared. One major mistake Schneider had seen was how companies confused supporting roles, like legal, human resources, and information technology, with product creation roles like design and development. Product creators are the true talent of any corporation, especially one claiming to bet on innovation. The other roles don't create products and should be there to serve those who do. A classic betrayal of this idea is when the IT department dictates to creatives what equipment they can use. If one group has to be inefficient, it should be the support group, not the creatives. If the supporting roles, including management, dominate, the quality of products can only suffer.

Mullenweg and Schneider shared a passion for creating a company that never betrayed these basic sensibilities. They wanted to hire only people who knew how to make great products and build a structure around them to let them to do their best while staying out of their way as much as possible. The autonomy of the volunteer WordPress community mapped well to this ideal, and they both reinforced it as the core ethos of Automattic. They wanted to avoid hierarchy, bureaucracy, and anything else that interfered with talented people doing their best work.

The single-sentence vision for WordPress had always been to democratize publishing, which meant they wanted anyone, anywhere, who had something to say to always be able to publish it for free. But values aren't something you have; they're something you use. Anyone can proclaim to believe in anything. The question is how much of their actions reflect those beliefs. The open source nature of WordPress and the free cost of WordPress.com ensured those values would be upheld for a long time. And Automattic often participated in demonstrations for free expression. In January 2011, when the threat of a federal bill referred to as the Stop Online Piracy Act threatened free speech, WordPress.com blanked out its entire front page, participating in protest with dozens of other websites. Mullenweg continually invested in ways to protect free speech online through the policies of WordPress but also by his participation in the industry at large. As a writer, I found it moving to work somewhere that invested heavily in the idea of free expression.

When I was hired in August 2010, I was the fifty-eighth employee. WordPress was used by 20 million blogs, and almost half of those were hosted on WordPress.com. Realizing how critical the values he'd learned for WordPress were to the culture he wanted to continue at Automattic, he wrote a creed that would appear on official documents, including in my offer letter:

> I will never stop learning. I won't just work on things that are assigned to me. I know there's no such thing as a status quo. I will build our business sustainably through passionate and loyal customers. I will never pass up an opportunity to help out a colleague, and I'll remember the days before I knew everything. I am more motivated by impact than money, and I know that Open Source is one of the most powerful ideas of our generation.
>
> I will communicate as much as possible, because it's the oxygen of a distributed company. I am in a marathon, not a sprint, and no matter how far away the goal is, the only way to get there is by putting one foot in front of another every day. Given time, there is no problem that's insurmountable.

It was the nicest-looking and simplest offer letter I'd ever seen. All of the legal verbiage was marked with HTML tags saying

<Legalise> and </Legalise>, which made me smile. It wasn't the product of a cold, disinterested lawyer-dominated bureaucracy. Instead, my offer felt like a letter from a real person who cared about the details and had a sense of humor. It was a nod to the culture in a place I'd never expect to find it. Unlike proclamations about culture that are easy to put in speeches and e-mails, it's the small decisions that define a culture. While I had my suspicions of any creed for any organization because they're easy to ignore, I was eager to work on a culture of my own: the culture of my team.

CHAPTER 5

YOUR MEETINGS WILL BE TYPED

On Friday August 24, the last day of my tour in Happiness, I had my first team meeting. It was the worst kind of meeting—the kind where no one knows why they're there. Mike, Beau, and Andy, my three programmers, had other projects and no room for new assignments. And then there was me with only one assignment—an assignment I was unavoidably overeager about after watching from the Happiness support sidelines for three weeks, of trying to make the team feel like a team. The last nail in the coffin was the fact that while other teams had clear directives, (Team Happiness was about customer support and Team NUX was about new users), Team Social's charter was the broadest of all. We had a long list of existing projects, plus pending decisions on what to do with projects everyone was finishing. The unwelcome bonus nail in this coffin of a meeting—a nail so definitive it rendered the meeting unsavable even by a nuclear-powered crowbar—was my choice to lead an around-the-room-introduction, the soul-draining death knell of millions of unloved meetings throughout history. The only good news was the meeting was short, which is never a mistake. Until the day you end a meeting where someone other than you says, "Wait! Can we meet longer?" it's safe to assume the meeting was longer than necessary.

Since each of us was hundreds of miles apart, we met using IRC, the company standard for meetings on the rare occasions they happened. IRC stands for Internet relay chat and in software terms it's a relic, a program created in 1988. It was funny that a young company like Automattic would use software so old, but to see the humor required being old enough to know how old IRC was (1988 was close to the year many Automatticians were born). It was so old to them that its age was unnoticed, much like how, when lying down in a park, you don't stop to think how old the dirt beneath you is. I avoided any "when I was your age" rants, as I had clear memories of being the young guy on a team hearing those rants. The culture was not going to fit to me; I had to fit in, at least for now.

Most people doubt online meetings can work, but they somehow overlook that most in-person meetings don't work either. Being online does mean everyone might be distracted, but plenty of meetings today are filled with people with their laptops open, messaging each other about how bored they are. My theory on meetings was simple: if what is being discussed is important, people will pay attention. Even at the universe's dullest company, if I called a meeting to decide who will get a 50 percent raise, I would have their full attention. There is nothing wrong with the concept of a meeting. If the people in a meeting think it's a waste of time, then either they're the wrong people or what's being discussed is not important enough to justify a meeting. I knew if I kept our meetings on important decisions and little else, we'd do fine, whether in person or online.

Meetings in IRC was simple. It's the same idea as using instant messaging or text messaging on your phone. If you have something to say, you type it. When you hit Return, others can see it. That's it. From a list of possible channels, you pick one, and a window opens. If other people are in the same channel, you see a list of their names. Our channel was called #social. The Happiness channel was called #happiness. We'd leave the IRC application open all day in the background so if anyone had a question or wanted to chat, we were available. For meetings, we'd pick a time, and everyone just showed up online. If someone was late, I'd ping them in Skype. It was very straightforward and simple. If you needed uninterrupted time, you could set everything to say you were busy.

A company rule was that anyone could join any channel. There were no passwords or restrictions. Often you'd see people on other teams lurking in your channel. And even if you didn't see them, everyone understood that all of the channels were logged, meaning you could go to an internal website and find a searchable history of every conversation ever held in IRC in the company. This seemed extreme to me at first, but I realized every corporation in America has the right to look at employee e-mails. Corporate communications are corporate property. At least at Automattic, the rules were clear and fair: everyone, not just executives, had access. Mullenweg and Adams explained to me the company line that if anyone missed a conversation or was new to the company, he or she could go back and see the actual discussion. This was one of many practices inherited from the WordPress open source project itself. The trade-off seemed to be the fact that knowing that they were being recorded changed what people were willing to say. I'd never seen a company with a policy like this, and I decided I'd have to wait and see if that were true.

The radical combination of remote work, IRC meetings, and transcripts reaffirmed something I'd always known: starting a new job makes you a paratrooper. You jump out of the safe, comfortable airplane of your past experience to land in a place you have seen only rough maps of—maps made by the people who most want you to jump. These maps are happier and neater than the landscapes they represent, yet you want the map to be true, so you trust it. As a result, most paratroopers, and new employees, never quite land where or how the plan says they will; it's just a question of who realizes that first. Once when taking a new job in a different group at Microsoft, I learned after I'd sent a broadcast e-mail to both groups announcing the move that the job I was told was mine no longer existed. Whoops. At least at Automattic, even in the confusion of my first day as a team lead, I had successfully landed somewhere.

With the paratrooper metaphor in mind, I prepped myself for landing at Automattic before I arrived. I made my own list of assets:

- I've led many different kinds of projects.
- I'm good at making decisions and designing things.
- I'm a good communicator.
- I have an excellent BS detector.

And my liabilities:

- I haven't done this in seven years.
- I've never worked on an open source project.
- I'm not a WordPress expert.
- I'm not a programmer.
- I won't be talking to people face-to-face.

Of my liabilities, the last one concerned me the most. The talent that had saved me in tough situations was conversation. That sounds corny, and it is. I'm finally old enough to accept that sometimes the hard truth isn't impressive or cool, but is dopey, corny, or boring. In every tough spot I've been in at work, the ace in my pocket was the ability to pull people aside and connect. If someone was upset, falling behind, or angry, I'd privately start an honest conversation. Either I'd finally shut up and listen and understand, or I'd say something that helped move things forward. At Automattic, that asset was gone. I couldn't go down the hall, drop into someone's office, and close the door. It was the only part of working remotely that scared me. I didn't think Skype could be quite the same, but I knew I'd have to try.

During my tour in support, I revised these lists often. I made another list of what my priorities should be. Making lists is a great way to clarify thinking. You put down thoughts, refine them, order them, and even share them with other people. And if you're willing to do the hard work of putting a list in priority order, you can condense great visions into a few simple sentences. The first thing I tell teams of people who are struggling is ML: Make a list. Write down the list of problems to solve or issues to fix. Get it out of their brain and on paper. It's less stressful when its written down. Then put them in order of importance, with an order that everyone understands: what comes first, what comes next, and so on. Making good ordered lists is the fundamental thing any effective leader does, and it's the heart of popular planning methods like Kanban and SCRUM.

Over my first few weeks, my list of priorities slowly fell into order. One item kept rising to the top, and many of the other things on the list weren't possible until that one item was successful. My list of priorities looked like this:

- Trust is everything.

Whatever grand vision I had for Team Social was unlikely to get far if Beau, Adams, and Peatling didn't trust me. They'd just met their new boss, and while I was granted implicit trust because Mullenweg had hired me, that wouldn't last if they decided I was a moron.

Reading it now it sounds like a cliché. It's not as if millions of workers around the world would have an epiphany if they read my list and say, "Trust? Oh, I thought it was *good* to stab colleagues in the back, which is why I've thrown so many under the wheels of my promotion-fueled bus." I know trust is obvious, but despite its obviousness it's rare. Clichés are often clichés because they're true (which is a cliché about clichés). They're easy to dismiss because they're well worn, but that's a mistake. Love and happiness are rare, despite the popularity of those words. We like to believe what we need is a huge breakthrough, a grand idea we've never heard before. This is a mistake. Knowing and doing are far apart. The reason most managers aren't good at what they do is that they overlook the basics, which likely includes earning the trust of their coworkers. Trust is expensive to build and easy to destroy, which is why it's rare. Given my liabilities, I bet on patience. It was the only way to develop the respect I needed to lead. The first meeting was a mistake because I was too eager and not patient enough.

One trick is to be the scribe. If you take on the task of taking notes, people have a chance to see how you think. If they find your recording of what happened clear and honest, you get a trust point. If the way you summarize complex things is concise but still accurate, you get another. Soon there's enough trust to lead decisions and take bigger bets. Being the scribe is often seen as a chore, but it has big upsides, especially in a supremely informal culture like Automattic's.

Of course, there were no official scribes at Automattic. The logging of IRC was meant to remove the need for summary e-mails and formal processes that bog down organizations. Instead, tools are chosen to put power in the hands of individuals and keep work democratic. And it should be no surprise as a company built on blogging that blogs themselves would make up a huge part of company communication. A special blog theme, called a P2, was made for this purpose.[1] This theme was so popular in the company that it became the primary name for internal blogs. Instead of saying, "Can you post that on my project's blog?" you'd say, "Can you post that on the P2?" It's the only WordPress theme I've seen with a name that took precedence over the blog itself. The name P2 came from "Project Log." When Joseph Scott and Matt Thomas, the programmer and designer who worked on it, needed a directory to put their work in, they called it Prolog. When the second version released, the name simplified to P2.

The way a P2 worked was simple and clever (it was similar to Basecamp, a communication tool made by 37signals). Anyone visiting a P2 in their browser would see a big box at the top. If they had a question, an idea, or a complaint, they could type something in that box and hit Submit. When they did, the message would appear in the list below. It was that simple. Any of those posts could be commented on by anyone and referenced by its own URL. Inspired by Twitter, the design was lightweight and fast. Since it was built on WordPress, it was easy to add features or make customizations.

When the teams were formed in August, each team created a new P2. It was the simplest way to signify a team existed at all. It was the primal claim to existence for anyone in WordPress world: I have a blog; therefore I exist. Beau created the Team Social P2 but left it generic. Other teams began the ancient tribal branding rituals of choosing colors and symbols, which was to be expected. Adams, whom I had barely met at this point, took a stab at giving our team its first branding. He wasn't a designer by even the most liberal definition, so this effort was brave. He made a joke out of our team's name in a darkly comic way, using the Soviet Union's hammer and sickle, now symbols of oppression, as the centerpiece of our P2 theme. It was a play on the word *social*: rather than just mean social media, it mean socialism. Aesthetics aside, Adams raised a flag for our team to the company showing we had a sense of humor, however twisted.

Communication at Automattic was roughly broken down as follows:

1. Blogs (P2): 75 percent
2. IRC: 14 percent
3. Skype: 5 percent
4. E-mail: 1 percent

Of course, since Skype and e-mail were private, these are just guesses. Most of the uses of e-mail, as low as it was, were for notifications about new posts or comments on P2s. I'd eventually take to e-mailing people individually on my team once a month to ask deeper questions about their performance and mine. But for day-to-day work, it was all P2, IRC, and Skype. P2s were much more than just for documenting meetings. Brainstorming, bug reports, discussions, rants, and jokes all found their primary home on the more than fifty-six P2s across the company. Several central P2s for human resources and a social P2 for watercooler-type conversations were also created, the latter becoming one of the most active.

After my lame meeting, I made one of the first posts on our P2. It was a flag to the company and to ourselves that we existed:

August 25, 2010

Team social had its first team chat yesterday and it's a good time to explain what we're about.

1. Our goal is to keep wp.com users happy and active.
2. We see better social tools as an excellent way to increase happiness and activity, but there are other ways and we'll be looking at them too. We want to be careful not to confuse one kind of means (social media thingies) with the ends (active/happy).
3. We expect to work in sweet harmony with Team NUX—they're focused on new user experience, and

we're focused on existing/ongoing user experience. For the user it should all be seamless and wonderful.

4. Our team is new—devs are still wrapping up other projects. We also have housekeeping to do on existing features in need of some love.

5. Our first sprint is focused on improving IntenseDebate, to get it in good shape so we can focus on other projects. You can always find our active sprint in the top of our P2 sidebar over there→

6. Here are our high level priorities for thinking about new ideas. I bounced these off Matt and they may be suitable as general purpose priorities:

   1. Improve user experience for users
   2. Increase market share
   3. Provide competitive advantage
   4. Generate revenue

7. We now have a list of known feature ideas or requests. This is currently a raw list pulled from the P2—we'll be adding to/discussing this as a team as we get going, to figure out future projects.

That's all for now. Questions/Feedback/Ideas welcome.

No one left a single comment. Had anyone read it? Did their lack of commentary mean anything? I didn't know. I'd have to look at what was happening on the other P2s to get a sense for what to expect or inquire with my teammates via Skype. By far the most significant item was #7. I'd taken the mess of dozens of features ideas we'd inherited and put them in a single list. Next would be to put that list in order based on the goals from #6. With an ordered list and buy-in from my team, we'd have clear goals and a way to filter out low-priority distractions. I'd judge my performance based on the quality of what we shipped, and what we shipped would be determined by the order of items on that list.

Learning from other P2s was a challenge. There were fifty-two of them. Mullenweg and Beau both suggested I use something called Jabber, a notification tool that acted like a switchboard, taking in updates from P2s, and provided filters for how and when I wanted alerts. I hated it. With the default settings on, it interrupted me every few minutes, inspiring a merciless uninstall. Had I been willing to spend time customizing it, perhaps it would have worked, but I am decidedly in the low-information camp. I did not believe in multitasking unless I was doing something trivial, a state I wanted to avoid. An ordinary coworker making an ordinary post on an unimportant P2 should never interrupt me. I wanted to pull low-priority information to me when I was interested in it rather than having it pushed. Anything my team was doing was high priority, but the rest of the company was low priority to me then.

I discovered a better way to manage P2s. Buried in the internal tools website was a single automated listing of every P2 post and comment, listed by most recent first. Each entry showed who made the post, when, which P2 it was from, and more. I looked at this a few times every day, keeping it in a separate tab, hitting Refresh, and then scrolling through an inventory of the company's entire communications since the last time I looked. I opened entries that were interesting in a separate browser tab, read the conversation, and left comments if appropriate. Few people consumed P2s this way, but it worked best by far for me. Mullenweg claimed to read every post and comment, not in real time, but he'd catch up every week or so. I couldn't see wanting to do this, much less achieving it even if I did.

Later on the day I made my first P2 post, Mullenweg and CEO Toni Schneider held the monthly town hall meeting. Mullenweg did these from wherever in the world he was, and in this case he was in San Francisco, allowing Schneider to join. The goal of the town halls was to provide direct access to Mullenweg for everyone and to let him share any news. Sometimes it was about new partnerships. Other times it was about new people he'd hired.

Any major milestones, press coverage, or other events he wanted to make sure we were aware of and understood would come up. He'd spend the first ten or thirty minutes with big news and then open the floor for Q&A.

To support the remote nature of these town halls, they used a combination of remote cameras and IRC. Mullenweg would set up a webcam on his laptop, and the rest of us would join two different IRC channels: one for posting questions to Matt and the other for employees to have side chats while Matt spoke. Each of us could be anywhere in the world, and the meetings would work exactly the same. At this August town hall, he talked mostly about the newly formed teams and the intent to make everyone more autonomous and productive. The company meeting was scheduled for September in Seaside, Florida, and he confirmed details about those plans. There were also questions about revenue and company strategy. Many of the questions were softballs, but there were a couple of bold ones. The IRC channel was filled with many jokes, sarcastic commentary, and links to references about whatever Matt said. It was a lively and free bunch, with thirty-five of the sixty employees tuning in. I found I could work while listening to the town hall in the background, shifting focus when I heard something interesting. I assumed many of the others were doing the same.

The only substantive instruction from the town hall was for us to work in two-week cycles. This was new for the company. Until this decree, everyone launched new features whenever they felt they were ready. This new mandate meant there was a time box: programmers would now be expected to work together and ship on schedule. In my project management brain, this was smart but challenging. Picking projects of the right size to fit into two weeks is hard if you don't estimate, and schedules that short preclude estimates. The intent was to force us to work incrementally, shipping what we had, and doing another two-week cycle on the project if needed. But Mullenweg gave few details about sorting it all out. This ambiguity was by design: he wanted each team to do its own experiments on how to make this work, giving the company the benefit of many different approaches.

Watching the town hall, I felt reassured. As different as this place was, the fundamentals were the same. Watching the chatter in the IRC channel filled me in on the personalities of the many people I hadn't yet met. Who was typing more? Who was silent? Who asked insightful questions? Who asked lame ones? Everyone's personality was on display as if we were doing the town hall live and in person. After the town hall, I felt confident that I could connect with my team and work out a plan. This was a place we could do great work. The doors were open.

In a few weeks, I'd get to work with my team in person at Seaside and meet much of the company for the first time. I was looking forward to it. I spent much time thinking about what I needed to do when I'd be together with my team. It wasn't clear how often I'd get to work with them in person, and being new to distributed teams meant Seaside would be precious time for us.

CHAPTER 6

THE BAZAAR AT THE CATHEDRAL

The 2010 company meeting was held in September at the beautiful village of Seaside, nestled into the rolling beaches of the northwest Florida coastline. Robert S. Davis, the town founder, had decided in 1979 to invent an old beach town on his vacant property. He hired architects to design buildings and homes in the weathered, rustic style found in older places up the coast. Seaside is where the film *The Truman Show*, a movie about a man in a television show where everyone knows it's a show but him, was made, and it's a brilliant matching of a movie and a location.

When I walked alone on the neat rows of upscale beach homes and past well-kept artisan shops, I couldn't shake the sense I was being watched. Everything seemed too neat, too perfect, and too ordered. My discomfort arose from the committee-driven aesthetic, as beautiful as it was, with colors, styles, homes, and shops conforming to the detailed rules of the town founders. In much the same way homes in *Architecture Digest* are beautiful but cold, the town sacrifices vibrancy for beauty. There is a master plan for everything—a plan conceived by the all-knowing architects. The single pub closes at 10:00 p.m., and noise ordinances are enforced after dark. I'm too much of a hooligan to feel I belong somewhere this tidy, but I'm in the minority, as thousands of people happily travel there every summer. The only reason Automattic was able to rent space for the company meeting was the timing: mid-September is the offseason for the beach crowd, and the recent BP oil spill in the Gulf of Mexico kept many away from the region.

As a venue for Automattic, Seaside is a fantastic cultural comparison. It's a town that believes primarily in control: it has used tightly held rules to construct the community. Automattic has most of the same values as the WordPress community, believing in autonomy, self-selection, and volunteerism. However opposed these philosophies seem, they're both unusual enough to provoke questions from experts about what the word *real* even means. Is Seaside a real town? Is Automattic a real company? Lazy critics dismiss new ideas with critiques like, "It's nice, but not real," or, "It can't scale," suggesting that if you developed the idea further, it would fail. But they forget to ask the bigger question: What good is something that scales well if it sucks? Why is size the ultimate goal or even a goal at all? If you're the kind of person who loves Seaside or the place where you work, you don't need it to be any bigger than it is. The inability to scale is one of the stupidest arguments against a possibly great idea: greatness rarely scales, and that's part of what made it great in the first place.

Before I could explore Seaside and Automattic's company meeting, I first had to escape the airport, which was strangely empty when I arrived. I found a driver waiting for me: a large, quiet man with a beard, holding up a sign with my misspelled name. As we walked outside, he told me not to expect any cheerleaders, which I thought was an odd thing to say. I looked at him curiously, wondering if perhaps he thought I was someone else or that this is one of those things kidnappers mention before they put a sack over your head. But he explained, as he pointed to the enormous black bus waiting outside, that he had just dropped off an entire troop of competitive cheerleaders and didn't have time to pick up a smaller car. I'd have to sit for the hour drive to Seaside in a vehicle built for forty people with nary a cheerleader or kidnapper to keep me company. My odd conveyance was unique, a penalty for arriving a few days late. Had I arrived with the rest of the company, I would have been paired with other folks from Automattic, cramming into a car or van together like a bunch of poor but happy college students for a fun trip to start the week. Sitting alone, feeling awkward in the empty space, I couldn't help but imagine it filled with merry Automatticians catching up, telling stores, and sharing those laughs you can only share with people you work with every day. It was an anticlimactic arrival. I felt lonely and out of place—the new guy arriving late to the party.

After the drive, Beau helped me find where Team Social was staying: a well-decorated condominium looking over a beautiful courtyard. The main square of Seaside was a network of three- and four-story buildings, each with sloping terraces, wide porches, and lookout towers with views to the ocean. Many were designed in distinctive styles, from Victorian to postmodern, and it was hard not to be impressed with how well these ideas blended together. Even the condo chosen for us had a beautiful patio with wide glass doors and a certain upscale beach town charm. I quickly dropped off my bags and joined Beau and the rest of the company in one of the large houses the company had rented.

Inside we found what was either a lively party or a rowdy meeting. It was hard to tell at first what it was. The room was full of waves of laughter and friendly debates. Some were working at laptops and others were drinking and playing, but the mix showed they wanted to be together in the same place regardless of what they were doing. It was one enormous room, stretching from a wide kitchen to a twelve-person dining table, out through to a multicouch living room. Nearly thirty people were there, and I assumed they were all Automatticians, but since I'd met only a few, it was hard to be sure. It looked more like a party at a very nice but geeky college dorm. Most people looked to be in their mid-twenties, and those who looked older dressed and behaved as if they too were that age.

The vibe of positive energy and camaraderie was undeniable, and I looked for an opening to find my way in. Beau slipped away, but I quickly spotted some familiar faces. Hanni gave me a warm smile and a friendly hug. For someone who looked so young, she has a wickedly sharp sense of humor and a reputation for destroying computer gear (her laptop was still in working order when I arrived). Zè, who had trained me during support, waved and nodded knowingly, as he, with his mastery of six languages, was prone to do. He was one of the older people at the company, and its primary linguist, managing the translation of WordPress into dozens of languages, a tough and often thankless job. It was the first time I'd met them in person since they trained me weeks ago, but that distinction was irrelevant. We had inside jokes and references just like any other officemates would. Andy Peatling helped me find a beer in the well-stocked communal fridge, and I was quickly introduced to some folks I hadn't met before. The kitchen overflowed with potato chips, granola bars, fruit, and a well-stocked bar sprawled out over a counter. I'd arrived, and with a drink in hand, I became part of the gang. Soon there was music and dancing, and I watched Peatling film Mike Adams showing off his amazing moves, perhaps for future team blackmailing and bribery. Sara Rosso from the VIP team joined in, proving that at least two Automatticians could dance.

Later that evening I found Lance Willet, the lead for Team Theme. I'd met him before briefly and found him to be smart and friendly, another talented and good-natured Automattician. He'd established a great reputation for himself as a theme developer, customizing WordPress for client websites. Soon he was on Mullenweg's radar and was hired a year or so before I was. Team Theme would soon become one of the best at the company, with Lance's combination of leadership and management setting good examples. That night I was fishing for advice, playing my "new guy at the company card" before it expired. Lance knew I'd managed many projects before and said only one thing, with a big smile: "Welcome to Chaos." He meant there were few rules here, and the ones that existed changed quickly. He thought I'd do fine, but that the best results would require commitment to improvisation.

It was fantastic advice. Had he tried to give me specifics, they likely would have been wrong by the time I tried to use them.

As the evening progressed, I realized there were some things I did not see at all:

- Name tags
- Schedules
- Projectors
- Reading packets
- Forms
- Surveys
- Flip charts

Most of the staples for the typical company retreat were nowhere to be found. Self-organization was assumed. Some basic instructions had been given and plenty of tools and support, but the majority of details were for each employee to decide. The early Automattic ideals of separating the supporters from the makers was in effect in Seaside. There was energy vibrating through the room. Everyone was fully present and engaged, ready for anything.

What's sad is that right now, as you read this, there are hundreds of similar organizational off-sites and retreat meetings happening, and the thousands of people attending them have the same central, desperate struggle: to stay awake. The crushing boredom that plagues these events is a disease born of good intentions gone wrong. No manager wants to bore people; they just can't help themselves, and the bureaucracies they work in make it worse. Event planners crush curiosity under the weight of agendas, topic lists, working groups, and exercises, all crammed together like a bad, hyperactive vacation. The slippery slope toward misery starts with all major players having their own agenda, their own thing they're championing this quarter, and they push to make it part of the official schedule. And as their peers respond in kind, a series of endless slices are made into every day, and every hour, until there is no room to breathe. And nothing is real. There is no actual work being done. Instead it's all metawork, or discussions about future work. It's a sea of abstraction. The nonmakers are in charge of the makers and insist on spending the off-site not making anything.

At some moment in every boring organizational off-site, everyone senses something is missing, but since this is like most other retreats they've been to, they can't imagine a better alternative. The result is that everyone arrives intending to practice the same skills they learned in elementary school of paying just enough attention during the day that they don't get called on much, so they can use the rest of their time in sessions to daydream about something meaningful. They appreciate the escape from the daily grind, but otherwise there's little upside to these events in spite of their expense.

The big bet of many retreats is the location. The hope is that a resort in the woods or a trip to a special city will provide a fresh environment away from the daily routines, a change that stimulates new thinking. But they forget the most important thing that location cannot change: the company culture. No matter where they go, they take dozens of forgotten assumptions about how work is done along with them. The more an event is driven by the people in power, the more it will reinforce the status quo. This is why these big meetings start with promises of growth and innovation and end with a vague sense of disappointment. Somehow the stakes are low, which means that if the results are poor, no one minds. There will be no firings or demotions for running a bad off-site.

Because Automattic is a distributed company, the meet-up has great significance: it's the only week all year that all employees are in the same place. From the typical executive's perspective, this puts even greater pressure on planning the week down to every second. There are good reasons to schedule presentations on what competitors are doing or to have leaders give strategic briefings. But little of this happens for Automattic. Instead of more structure, more chaos is introduced. Instead of an escape or a heavily scripted show, the company meet-up focuses on launching new ideas on WordPress.com—not for practice but for real. Every team was instructed to pick a project for the week and ship it before they went home.

The work at Seaside was similar to how work was done year round at Automattic. The main difference was that we could all work in the same space if we so chose (which most did). The general way work was done was simple. If you are a programmer, you write code. If you are a designer, you design things for programmers to make or you make it yourself. That's it. Since WordPress.com is a service, it can be updated any time, day or night. The burden of deciding when to launch something is on the maker, not a marketer. If something is launched or a bug is fixed, data is instantly collected about how it's used, which serves as the basis to make quick revisions. There are no big schedules, few big plans, and no enforced mechanisms for coordination. It sounds like chaos, and it is. But if everyone understood chaos and perhaps liked the uncertainty, they would find freedom and opportunity. And if everyone wanted to do great work, they'd seek out collaborators and greater order when needed. The move to teams was supposed to encourage this to happen more often.

Most people can't imagine working this way. I'd certainly done it before on some projects, but I'd never seen an entire company do it all at the same time. For a small team, autonomy is freedom, but with fifty or more, soon you have people getting in your way.

The general work flow at Automattic had seven steps:

1. *Pick a problem.* A basic problem or idea for WordPress.com is chosen. It could be something like, "It's too hard to print blog posts," or, "Let users share from WordPress to Facebook." There are always hundreds of ideas and dozens of opinions about which ideas are important. There's no formal system for deciding, but many came from Mullenweg or as suggestions

from the Happiness folks. After an idea is chosen, discussion begins on how it should work.

2. *Write a launch announcement and a support page.* Most features are announced to the world after they go live on WordPress.com. But long before launch, a draft launch announcement is written. This sounds strange. How can you write an announcement for something that doesn't exist? The point is that if you can't imagine a compellingly simple explanation for customers, then you don't really understand why the feature is worth building. Writing the announcement first is a forcing function. You're forced to question if your idea is more exciting for you as the maker than it will be for your customer. If it is, rethink the idea or pick a different one.

3. *Consider what data will tell you it works.* Since it's a live service, learn from what users are doing. The plan for a new feature must consider how its positive or negative impact on customers can be measured. For example, if the goal is to improve the number of comments bloggers get from readers, we'd track how many comments visitors write each day before and after the change.

4. *Get to work.* Designers design. Programmers program. Periodically someone checks the launch announcement to remind everyone of the goal. As more is learned about what's possible, the announcement becomes more precise. Sometimes the feature pivots into something different and better.

5. *Launch.* When the goal of the work has been met, the feature launches. It's often smaller in scope than the initial idea, but that's seen as a good thing. The code goes live, and there is much rejoicing.

6. *Learn.* Data is captured instantly and discussed, often hourly, by the folks who did the work. Bugs are found and fixed. For larger features, several rounds of revisions are made to the design.

7. *Repeat.*

Since the company started in 2005, it had launched hundreds of features and improvements this way. Many people had never worked at a major software company before, and this was the most elaborate development process they'd seen.[1] Do you see anything missing? If you've made a product in your life, I'm sure you did. What about marketing? Where is user experience design? What about quality assurance? What about collisions between different projects? There are dozens of things this process doesn't account for. Any mature company would look at this process and laugh, and with some good reason. But what they'd miss is the power of simplicity. A simple process affords three things:

1. It is easy to launch projects.
2. If it's easy to launch, small projects will get launched.
3. If small things are launched, there is a fast feedback loop about what worked and what didn't, which can be quickly improved because of #1.

The fundamental mistake companies that talk about innovation make is keeping barriers to entry high. They make it hard to even try out ideas, blind to how much experimentation you need to sort the good ideas from the bad. I've visited companies that use big meetings, with far too many cooks in the room, to rank ideas based on one-sentence descriptions. It was madness. While few at Automattic had ever experienced this, their process was on the other end of the spectrum: they had faith in the future. If a feature launched and had value, the missing things could be addressed later. And if after launch it didn't have value, few would use it and it could be killed (although I'd learn later that killing of experiments was far too rare).

More than anything else, I recognized that the big cultural bet wasn't on process but on people. Instead of betting on the enforcement of an elaborate fifty-step process or the magical talents of management, Automattic put the onus on individuals. It was like a small start-up company where every employee was empowered, out of necessity, to make many decisions free of approvals from a long list of grumpy corporate gatekeepers. For me, and all the places I'd been, Automattic seemed liberating. All I had to worry about was Team Social. If we did good work, the rest was easy. I didn't have to navigate the stormy seas of an angry, swirling bureaucracy threatening to sink good ideas before they'd even had a chance.

Before we left for Seaside, we chose something called Hover-cards as Team Social's project. The goal was to make a business card of information appear whenever a visitor to a blog moved the mouse over a person's name. Why we didn't call the feature "business cards" or "identity cards," something in plain English, is beyond me now. Gravatar was the brand name for Automattic's free web identity service, which instantly made your profile image appear in comments or blog posts just by typing in your e-mail address. Although millions of people used the service, few knew its name, and it was silly to cram it in. It's always a bad idea to name things after how they work or to fit into brand strategy. The best feature names simply describe what the thing does.

The idea itself was straightforward, and other websites had done it. We even had a basic design that Isaac Keyet, the lead of Team Mobile, had sketched months ago. I wrote the launch announcement before we left, and by time I'd arrived late in Seaside, Beau, Andy, and Mike had much of it working: enough to demonstrate it for me when I arrived. We joked about how they could have spent the time before I'd arrived goofing off or doing work and that they decided to do work, which was good for me. With our head start, we could go play, and off we went in search of other folks with fun on their minds.

CHAPTER 7

THE BIG TALK

The entire company stood out in the hot sun, assembled on the long grass lawn of Seaside's elementary school. It was time for the company tradition of taking a photo of all the employees. In the early years, this was easy, since there were fewer than a dozen people, but now with more than fifty to arrange, these photos were spatial jigsaw puzzles. Mullenweg, aka PhotoMatt, had scouted locations and realized the lawn was one of the few places that would work, since he could go upstairs at the school and take the photo looking down at the group. There he stood up on the third floor, one eye closed, the other looking through the viewfinder of his fancy camera. Below him was his small army of Automatticians, most of whom he had hired personally, but he was too busy to be proud. He called out the names of people who needed to move, and in what direction, to fit in the frame.

After long minutes of yelling down to the squinty-eyed crowd, he finally activated the preset he'd programmed into the camera. It started taking a photo every second as he ran down the stairs. The program was a clever insurance policy for guaranteeing at least one photo without someone's eyes closed, something he couldn't ensure from three stories below the camera. It also gave him the possibility of making a fun short movie from the combined photographs.

When he reached the ground floor, he scrambled to find his place in the front. Everyone looked up and smiled, cheering loudly.

Mullenweg yelled out instructions for people to wave their arms over their heads like at a rock concert, to flash the jokey WordPress gang sign (a W and a P made each made with one hand) and other poses. Finally, after all the ideas were exhausted, everyone cheered again and the crowd dispersed. People were happy to get out of the heat and get back to work on their team projects.

But just as the group was breaking up to walk away, someone spotted all of Team Social running from the far side of the field. It was an embarrassing run, since from the moment we were spotted, everyone knew the photos they'd just taken were ruined because our team was missing. While we felt bad about being late, somehow we collectively found the fact that we were the ones who had screwed things up entertaining. We were laughing and running at the same time. When Mullenweg realized what had happened, he was rightfully annoyed: we were out of time. Lunch was waiting. This meant the entire company would have to reschedule the photo for the next day. We apologized and quickly dispersed into the crowd, feeling bad but still giggling like a bunch of teenagers. We didn't know it then, but the pleasure in mischief we felt on that run would soon become a central part of our reputation.

The reason we were late was a good one: we were busy working. Four people is an excellent team size, and in these early days, before we had much chemistry, the ability to circle around a single laptop was a huge advantage. Working online together had been fine so far, but being in the same room together gave us a new energy. This was exactly what these meet-ups were meant to achieve: for us to learn things about working together we could reuse the rest of the year when working apart.

More interesting perhaps was the power of working on a four-person team. I joked with Mullenweg when he hired me that compared to managing large teams in large divisions, the idea of working with a team this small, in a company this tiny, seemed easy. Half the challenge of being a project manager is the things you must deal with that have nothing to do with your own team.

From fighting for resources to coordinating with other groups, the prospect of all my personnel responsibilities fitting in a car together was refreshing.

There are many theories about why teams of four to six work best, but the simplest is ego. With about five people, there's always enough oxygen in the room. It means on average that every person gets to speak once every five times, which is enough for everyone to feel they are at the center of things. At this level of participation, their pride can be invested in the team instead of focused inwardly on themselves. The US and other national armies made similar observations about the magic of small unit sizes, and it's the basis for how they've trained soldiers since 1948.[1] Larger groups were less likely to fire their weapons to defend themselves, but if they were trained in small units, their rates of fire increased. From this perspective, a team of ten to twenty people is unlikely to function in the same way as a small team does. It's likely that smaller units will naturally form despite what the organization chart says.

Having worked with these guys for only five weeks, and the fact that the Hovercard project was half built before I'd arrived, I had little to do. My feedback took minutes to hear, but an hour or more to implement. Even the bugs I found took far less time to explain to Adams or Peatling than it would for them to fix. If I'd arrived earlier, there'd be tasks to do, but there was nothing left. It was conceivable I could start learning PHP to help write code, but that would require getting someone on my team to set up my laptop for programming work, which would take hours. Besides, part of my experiment was to see if being a pure lead had value at Automattic. It was too early to give up on that notion.

I couldn't help but consider what Washington Roebling, one of the engineers of the Brooklyn Bridge, once wrote: "Man is after all a finite being in capacities and powers of doing actual work. But when it comes to planning, one mind can in a few hours think out enough work to keep a thousand men employed for years."[2]

I thought about this while I was sitting there and felt foolish. It'd be one thing if I took some pride in the design itself, the strongest skill set I could offer, but Isaac's was good. Sitting idle made me anxious, especially if I was around people who were working. It was an unusual feeling. I'd worked on many large, complex, stressful projects, yet here I was on a small one with nothing to do but read random P2s. I wasn't needed, and without anything to do, I couldn't help but consider Automattic didn't have a place for me after all.

Back when the web was new and the rest of Team Social was in junior high, I started my career at the beginning of the first browser wars. I worked on Internet Explorer 1.0 in 1995, a time when web browsers were so unimportant to the world that it didn't make it into the historic Windows 95 launch. Instead we were relegated to the Plus pack, the add-on people could buy if they wanted more screen savers. Screen savers! This obscurity is the hallmark of many important things. No one sees the importance until long after, and then they all share the same lie about the wave they saw coming way back when. No one expected what happened to happen.

The browser wars ran from 1995 to 1999, with Microsoft and Netscape fighting what was the fastest and most intense software battle of the era, perhaps in history. It was the birth of now common concepts like beta releases and Internet time, as suddenly software updates weren't annual events but quarterly or even weekly occurrences. And the browser software was free, changing the business models of software and services forever. It was an amazing time to be a kid out of school: I was given more responsibility than I deserved on an important project for the industry. I was only twenty-four years old in 1996, and I had a central role in how parts of Internet Explorer were made, soon leading the design and development of many features in Internet Explorer 3.0 to 5.0. Despite its clunky reputation today, Internet Explorer was good, fast, simple software back then—good enough to win reviews and fans.

For five years I did everything there was to do in leading a software project: designing, triaging, scheduling, recruiting, screaming, crying, and rejoicing with each alpha, beta, and final release. I prototyped features; collaborated with designers, engineers, and testers; and learned from people who were great at all of those things. I negotiated deals with CEOs, contributed at web standards groups, and went on stage in front of thousands to demonstrate work my team had done. Despite how large Microsoft was at the time, life on the Internet Explorer team was like a start-up. I was expected to do many different things and was given latitude in how I got them all done. Internet Explorer shipped every few months, something unheard of for software at the time (except, of course, for Netscape, the company that kicked Microsoft's ass so badly we had to ship fast to catch up).

As I watched Team Social work, happily uncontaminated by any pretense of management by me, I kept in mind the lesson I learned from Joe Belfiore, one of the best bosses I've ever had.

He told me the central way he'd evaluate me was the quality of what made it out the door. It wasn't about the ideas I had or how I managed schedules. It wasn't how I ran meetings or how well liked I was. Those were all secondary. What mattered was what we shipped. And he told me the only reason anything good ships is because of the programmers. They are everything. They are not factory employees; they are craftspeople, craftspeople who are the fundamental creative engine of making software. Although my job title was program manager, I wasn't granted power to run around making demands all day. There would be days I'd need to make demands, but I'd have to earn them. I had to earn the respect and trust from the programmers and designers I worked with. With trust, everything was possible. With trust, I could discover how to get the best possible work from them. But sitting in Seaside, watching my team put the finishing touches on Hovercards, I didn't have a chance to discover anything. And as the days at Seaside went on, I had to bite my tongue every time my ego came up with something to say or do to force myself into the center of the work. I knew it was a mistake. Patience was the only way to find the opportunities to be of use. But there was one thing I knew I couldn't be patient about: giving the Big Talk.

When a new team forms or the central project gets cancelled, there are lingering doubts on everyone's mind. And the more unusual the circumstances are, the bigger the doubts are. Leaders have two good choices with that uncertainty: use that tension to your advantage or diffuse the tension.

I'm the kind of leader who kills uncertainty. I want to identify the doubts and nail them to the wall. They might linger there for weeks, but by making everyone's private fears public, they become far less dangerous.

I got the others on Team Social together one night before dinner in the dining room in our Seaside apartment. Sitting there, it was as if we all lived together and were having a kind of awkward family meeting. The immaculate table, the kitchen, and the entire apartment made it seem unreal, almost as if we were on some kind of reality TV show about teams at start-ups. Pushing the strangeness of the situation out of my mind, I jumped right in.

I explained I knew full well that hiring me was an experiment. But I told them I liked experiments, and they should too. Experiments were awesome. The only way you learn is by doing things where you don't know the outcome. The only problem with experiments is not when the go wrong, but when you can't end them. I explained that Mullenweg and I had discussed the challenges. If any of the experiments we were doing, from teams to my leadership choices, to even the nature of my employment, didn't work out, they should let me or Mullenweg know. Either we'd fix it, or I'd leave. Until that happened, I was open to everyone's ideas for how our team should work.

It seems now like an odd conversation. But as awkward as it sounds, what I'd offered is the unspoken truth in any healthy organization. Every new manager is a kind of experiment. And any experiment that goes wrong should be changed. I can't recall ever reading a book on management that prescribed bringing this up directly, but it seemed obvious. If I couldn't earn trust in the Hovercard project, I had to find other turf to start with. More than anything else, I wanted them to know that whatever questions they had about me or our situation were valid and that I was thinking about them too. Bringing it up together surfaced those doubts so we could work out answers together. As the lead, I could raise these issues without being confrontational, whereas they could not. So I did it.

But I also made the argument for why it might work. I had experience with just about everything that goes right and wrong on projects and with teams. Much of that knowledge should be useful to Team Social, and it'd be up to us to figure out what it was, apply it, and then share what worked with the other teams. Part of the reason I was hired was to help define the role of a team lead for the company, not just for Team Social.

My last point was the singular way I'd evaluate my success: to get the best value for Automattic out of ever hour they worked. Every decision I was going to make as lead—what projects we worked on, what bugs we fixed, what questions we asked—would be about maximizing their value. Not every feature or bug fix had the same value to customers, and therefore to Automattic, and my role as lead was to keep the work on everyone's plate to have the greatest value possible. I expressed this in terms of how valuable their time was to me rather than them as a resource for me to exploit.

It all took less than five minutes, and when I finished, they didn't say much. Nothing seemed to faze them. These guys were smart and practical, and although they were appreciative of what I'd said, it didn't signify much to them at the time. Until I demonstrated these ideas with actions, they meant little. What was there to debate? They asked a question or two, which I answered, and then we were done. I couldn't speak for the rest of the company, but these guys were unflappable. Perhaps having lived in the autonomous Automattic world, they found my big talk far from surprising. With the chat over, we all got up together and went off to find some fun.

Before we left, though, I had two questions that had been on my mind that I asked them as group:

1. *How do you know if you're doing a good job?* They all shrugged simultaneously and I laughed. Unlike most corporations that emphasize performance evaluations, none of them were particularly concerned. It had never been an emphasized part of their experience at the company. It seemed to them like an odd question to even ask, given how rarely it came up with Mullenweg or Toni, or in the company at large. It was not a promotion-oriented culture. Instead they cared mostly about how much value they were getting out of the work.
2. *How should we handle within-team conversations on our P2?* I worried we'd be derailed by outsider opinions interrupting what should be conversations purely within our team. Peatling joked, "We 're comfortable blowing people off," and Adams and Beau

laughed in agreement. They meant they had strong filters for who was on the team and who wasn't, and opinions from random others wouldn't derail them. If they didn't mind, neither did I. Like a company that changes its floor plan from private offices to an open floor plan, public P2s didn't completely eliminate privacy; it just changed the rules.

At the end of our week at Seaside, all of the teams got up in front of the company to present their work. It felt great to stand in front of the company as a team and show what we'd put together. There were plenty of questions about Hovercards and how they'd work in different situations. Most of what I remember are the notable oohs and aahs as we did our demonstration, sounds I hadn't heard about software I'd worked on with a team of people for far too long.

CHAPTER 8

THE FUTURE OF WORK, PART 1

Books about the future of work make the same mistake: they fail to look back at the history of work or, more precisely, the history of books about the future of work and how wrong they were. Few visions of the future come true, as we're very bad at predicting much of anything. Can you guess what sentence will come next? Did you guess this one would have a flaming zombie banana in it, a fruit so horrific it crawls the earth forever, eating banana brains? If we can't guess the next sentence in a book, there's little hope of guessing the future. Failed predictions aside, a common presumption is that the future will be uniform and singular, discounting how chaotic the world is at any time. William Gibson famously wrote, "The future is here, it's just not evenly distributed."[1] But the past is unevenly distributed in the present too. At the same time we have poor families working on farms with their bare hands, urban organic chefs are heralded as innovators for using rustic cooking methods and college dropouts get venture capital funding for start-ups based on the centuries-old concept of to-do lists. There are so many kinds of work and the notions of the past and future are so circular that only a fool would confidently predict what's next.

I won't be making broad proclamations about riding jetpacks to the office, the productivity boons of Matrix-style neural implants, or how time travel helmets will improve profits (however, you can simulate time travel by jumping ahead to chapter 10, where, in the future of this book relative to where you are now, I just happen to be discussing time travel). But I can tell you what we can learn from what Automattic and similar companies have done. In this chapter, and twice more later in this book, I'll break from my story to review the lessons from my tale so far.

RESULTS TRUMP TRADITIONS

When you read any two books on the same subject, you realize there is more good advice than anyone can possibly apply. If you look at popular dilemmas like weight loss or seeking happiness, you can find equally reputable sources offering the opposite advice. Who's right? Even a singular source of advice can be hard to follow. A. J. Jacobs, in his book *The Year of Living Biblically*, set out to practice all the advice in the Old and New Testaments.[2] Despite his fanatical dedication, he discovered the task was impossible since the hundreds of commandments (the ten we know plus the 603 we've since dismissed) cannot be followed simultaneously.[3] Some contradict others. Some demand interpretation. The dozens of Judeo-Christian factions have their own lists of which to follow and which to ignore. The ultimate question of any advice, rules, or traditions is, What do you ignore and why? No one can ever follow it all. This is the **advice paradox:** no matter how much advice you have, you must still decide intuitively what to use and what to avoid. Even if you seek meta-advice, advice on which advice to take, the paradox still applies as you make the same choice about that advice too. Even if we try to hide inside the traditions of our elders, there is a universe of equally defensible alternatives followed by people with different elders than we have.

The gift of unusual organizations like Automattic is a reminder to open our minds. The problem with modern work, and one that sheds light on the future, is how loaded workplaces are with cultural baggage. We faithfully follow practices we can't explain rationally. Why is it that work has to start at 9:00 a.m. and end at 5:00 p.m.? Why are you required to wear a tie if you're a man and a skirt if you're a woman? Why are meetings sixty minutes long by default, and not thirty? We have little evidence these habits produce better work. Instead we follow these practices because we were forced to when we entered the workforce, and over time, they became so familiar we've forgotten they are merely inventions. All traditions are inventions; it's just a question of how old the invention is. There is nothing wrong with tradition until you want progress: progress demands change, and change demands a reevaluation of what the traditions are for and how they are practiced.

A central element in Automattic culture was results first.[4] Nobody cared when you arrived at work or how long you worked. It didn't matter if you were pantless in your living room or bathing in the sun, swinging in a hammock with a martini in your hand. What mattered was your output. Shouldn't the quality of work be the primary measure of worker performance? Isn't it good, then, to eliminate traditions that get in the way and add ones that help? Working distributedly facilitated this since many stupid traditions around work status, such as judging people by who arrives early or stays late, were impossible. You couldn't complain about who was in the corner office or had the reserved parking space. Instead, all you saw of your coworkers was the code they produced, the designs they made, the tickets they resolved, or the comments they wrote.

Some Automatticians worked from what are called coworking spaces, independently owned rentable offices designed for freelancers and remote workers.[5] These spaces provide a comfortable middle ground, retaining employee autonomy but giving people a social setting to work in. People who use coworking spaces often socialize together, providing the friendships and social structure many people need to stay productive. Automatttic offered employees a coworking stipend, another act of support for employees discovering how best to get work done.

Any manager who eliminates superfluous traditions takes a step toward progress. If removing a restriction improves performance or has no impact on performance but improves morale, everyone wins. Continuing tradition simply because it's a tradition works against reason. It assumes that five thousand years from now, if our species survives, we'll still be wearing shirts and ties and fighting through traffic to arrive at 9:00 a.m. Every tradition we hold dear was once a new idea someone proposed, tried, and found valuable, often inspired by a previous tradition that had been outgrown. The responsibility of people in power is to continually eliminate useless traditions and introduce valuable ones. An organization where nothing ever changes is not a workplace but a living museum.

Mullenweg had an exceptional ability to let things that do not matter slide, fueling a results-first culture. He read widely, studying what other people he admired did, yet he believed there are always simpler alternatives. Some of this stems from his personal experience. Dropping out of college is supposed to be a bad idea. Making software for free is unserious. Letting people work remotely is fanciful. WordPress's success in spite of convention has led to his, and the culture's, confidence that the best way to learn is to do—to think (but not for too long), make decisions, learn from what happens, and repeat. He saw little reason to debate things for weeks or build elaborate strategies. Instead he preferred experimenting, collecting data, and repeating. He also had great intuition for holistic thinking. He realized many experiments would fail but that experimentation was essential. WordPress or Automattic as systems would always benefit in the long run from the lessons learned from those attempts, including the failures.

The shift to teams at Automattic involved many simultaneous experiments. Many of the first leads were inexperienced. Some were unsure why they were chosen. Dozens of employees had never worked on teams before. I would have advised more coaching, but putting a trusted staff in the center of figuring it out was the fastest way to learn. They would work together in deciding what new habits were needed and what old habits needed to change.

CREATIVES VERSUS SUPPORTERS

The volunteer culture Automattic inherited from WordPress, where contributors were under no obligation to participate, defined a landscape that granted wide autonomy to employees. Schneider and Mullenweg went to great lengths to keep support roles, like legal, human resources, and even IT, from infringing on the autonomy of creative roles like engineering and design. The most striking expression of this is that management is seen as a support role. The company stays as flat as possible for this reason. Schneider described his philosophy in this way:

1. Hire great people.
2. Set good priorities.
3. Remove distractions.
4. Stay out of the way.

These freedoms at Automattic reminded me that the hardest part of work is what goes on between your ears and between you and your coworkers. The trends and gadgets that make up most conversations about the future of work miss the point. Instead of vice presidents seeing the problem as a lack of a tool or a secret method, they should realize they're in the way more than they realize. Granting authority is more powerful than any software, device, or method. Instead of treating employees like children, which many executive staffs do, Schneider and Mullenweg explicitly desired an environment for autonomous adults—a place for people who know best what they need to do great work.

To put my thoughts on the future of work another way, I'm often asked in my work as a writer what the best word processor is to use. My answer is always the same: your brain. Most people find this answer frustrating, but it's a sincere one. The hard parts cannot be mechanized. What makes a good filmmaker is not the camera he or she uses but how this person uses it, and the gear that works best for one person won't be best for someone else. This is true for all work that has any element of creativity. But people don't want to hear this. We want to believe in a singular universal solution we can buy, a faith we believe in, perhaps because most of us make livings selling other people products marketed on the false promise of those wishful thoughts.

An excellent example of staying out of the way is that when teams were formed at Automattic, a major question was how they should collaborate. At first everyone stayed with P2s, IRC, and Skype purely out of inertia, but soon teams, on their own, tried new things. One team switched to Skype video. Another tried Google Hangouts. There was no official mandate or policy. Each employee, and each team, decided which tools to try and which to keep. The tools were never of primary importance, although Toni and Matt made clear we had their support to buy the ones we needed and try them out. But what always mattered most was went on in each employee's mind. We were trusted to figure out which tools supported our work styles individually and as teams. There was never a mandate not to use e-mail. People simply found that the combination of P2s and IRC solved most needs, so that's what they used. Had a team wanted to try being e-mail-centric, it could have.

Even across the company, the freedom to try tools ruled. When Nick McCormick, a programmer on Team Janitorial, got frustrated with scanning in expense reports, he set up a company account with Expensify, a mobile app he found that lets users take photos of receipts on their phone and submit them. Other employees tried it, and soon it was the recommended tool. And if someone found something better, they'd have moved to that instead. I recognized these changes were easier in a company of fifty than five thousand, but to see these changes at all was inspiring.

HIRE SELF-SUFFICIENT, PASSIONATE PEOPLE

I did see things that would be serious problems at an ordinary company. But these issues were generally compensated for by the talents, passions, and collaborations of Automatticians. Watching coworkers at Seaside, their exuberance was undeniable. They'd do this work on their own time, for pleasure. In his classic book *The Soul of a New Machine*, Tracy Kidder noticed that Data General's efforts to hire people with strong internal motivations changed things: "Labor was no longer coerced. Labor volunteered. When you signed up you in effect declared, 'I want to do this job and I'll give it my heart and soul.'"[6]

Of course, the mission of WordPress to democratize publishing is easier to be passionate about than, say, cleaning toaster ovens. It's easier to find motivated people for some work than others. But I learned how little résumés and pedigrees express about a person's passion. It takes more passion to choose, on your own, to build a website, a mobile application, or a company than to follow years of instructions to get a degree. A GPA is not a strong indicator of passion, except for the dubious motivation of wanting to find right answers for other people's questions. Degree programs are highly structured and have the greatest appeal to people who depend on structure. Many Automatticians didn't study design or development in college, but instead learned their chops as solo web designers, jack-of-all-trade WordPress consultants, and other varied roles.

Many employees at Automattic were what's called T-shaped, meaning they had one very deep skill set, and a wide range of moderate proficiencies. Although I was hired as a lead, my deep skill set in this sense was interaction design. Diversity of skill makes people self-sufficient. They didn't need much help to start projects and were unafraid to learn skills to finish them. This self-sufficiency prevented the need for paternalistic management. They did not want to be coddled. They weren't afraid to get their hands dirty in tasks that in a mature engineering company would span the turf of three or four different job titles. That lack of specialization made people better collaborators since there was less turf to fight over. The culture valued results more than process: people were happy to lend expertise they had or teach others what they knew.

The game company Valve, makers of the games Half-Life and Portal, have a similar philosophy. They hire T-shaped programmers and designers—people who are masters at one craft but skilled at many. Valve also bets heavily on employee autonomy, going further than Automattic with its complete absence of formalized teams or hierarchy. Projects form at the whim of employees. Colleagues decide for themselves what projects to work on. Although the company is not distributed, employees' desks are on wheels, and they can choose for themselves what project they want to join, literally rolling down the hallway to become part of the project while it lasts. The Valve company handbook, leaked online in 2012, says, "We don't have any management, and nobody 'reports to' anybody else. We do have a founder/president, but even he isn't your manager. This company is yours to steer—toward opportunities and away from risks. You have the power to green-light projects. You have the power to ship products."[7]

When you're confronted with the choice, a job offering great power is polarizing. Some people find the sound of it liberating, while others find it scary. Most people who work for someone else don't really want this much responsibility. If they did, they'd start their own companies or be self-employed. The fact they're working for someone else represents a trade they're willing to make, sacrificing autonomy for security (as Kafka wrote, "It's often safer to be in chains than to be free"[8]). The trade-off that companies like Valve and Automattic offer is different. In some ways, the power they offer individual contributors is greater than what middle managers at large Fortune 500 companies have. However grand their executive jobs appear from the outside at these companies, their theoretical power is diminished by the bureaucracies their decisions must navigate through to have any impact at all.

Self-sufficient passionate people are hard to find. No manager puts up job postings that state "Wanted: infantile dullards with narrow abilities and fragile motivations." But like attracts like. Every time a company settles for a mediocre hire, it becomes harder to recruit the best. And just as Mike Little joined Mullenweg to start WordPress, finding the first match sets the tone. Once you have two or three like-minded people, a culture forms that attracts more people with similar values and repels those that don't.

Remote work is merely physical independence, and the biggest challenge people who work remotely face is managing their own psychology. Since they have more independence, they need to be masters of their own habits to be productive, whether it's avoiding distractions, staying disciplined on projects, or even replacing the social life that comes from conventional work with other friendships. The hire-by-trial approach Automattic uses filters out people not suited for remote work for whatever reason. It's fair to say many talented people aren't suited to remote work, but many are.

While few established companies can choose to become completely distributed, the distribution of Automattic, among its other interesting attributes, begs the question: What assumptions do you have about your organization that hurt you? And what experiments are you doing to discover them and find better ways to work?

CHAPTER 9

WORKING THE TEAM

After the company meeting at Seaside, Team Social gained momentum. We shipped several small features, fixed dozens of bugs, and put our massive list of feature ideas into order. To set a regular pace for ourselves, we agreed to the following:

Monday: Team meeting in IRC (10:00 a.m. PST, 6:00 p.m. for Peatling).

Monday: Everyone would be assigned an MIT (Most Important Thing) to work on.

Thursday: Everyone posts their status on our P2.

Friday: I post a summary to other leaders on the leads' P2. There was a special P2 just for team leads.

Monthly: I e-mail everyone for one-on-one questions about how they were doing.

IRC and P2 were the glue that held us together and made this simple spine of a structure work. This was the minimum amount necessary to function as a team, and it worked well. When it didn't, everyone understood I was granted nag powers and could pester people in Skype who were late with things. No one complained about my nagging, although given the short attention spans at the company, my nagging happened often. A trick of leading creative teams is finding creative ways to nag people. You get more mileage if you make people laugh, even if it's at themselves, at the same time you're reminding them of something they've forgotten.

Feeling good, I did some experiments of my own. I was invited to give a lecture in Chicago but didn't take time off from Automattic. Instead I worked on my laptop in various cafés and in my hotel lobby. Even when I had to go offline for a few hours, most of what my team had been up to was visible on our P2 and I could catch up easily. Unlike e-mail, where knowledge stays in people's inboxes, using P2s for most things a conventional company would use e-mail for meant the conversations persisted in a way I could skim, search, and contribute to. It was always assumed that people would drop in and out of being online. Since we rarely had short-term deadlines, it was okay for conversations to float over a day or two, whether they were on P2 or Skype. We all had the habit of leaving a note somewhere, often in our IRC channel, if we were going to be offline. I might ping Peatling in Skype with a question, and he'd respond an hour later, and then I'd reply that night. We all respected the need to be online at the same times when needed, but often it wasn't necessary.

Skype was the best indicator of who was around at any moment, but even when people were online, it could take minutes or an hour before they'd respond. The assumption was always that people were working in other windows and would respond when they could. This was a major reason text was more popular than voice: text chat leaves both parties free to do other things. Voice demands nearly complete attention from both parties. In Skype, a green light meant they were available and yellow that they were away from their machine (or wanted you to treat them as if they were away). IRC had similar status indicators for each employee, and sometimes I'd find one of them was busy in a chat room when my Skypes went unanswered. But everyone was easy to find there, sort of like looking for someone in the conference room if they weren't at their desk. Last resort was to ping them on their cell phone. I was told to be in IRC if I was working, because sometimes people were having conversations and would ping me to join in. None of this was complex or distracting. It was straightforward. Although chat rooms and blogs can be disasters on the Internet, at Automattic it was a contained universe. Everyone was respectful and good-natured.

A bigger experiment in the weeks after Seaside was my visit to the company main office in San Francisco. Automattic headquarters was in a beautiful open loft at Pier 38, right on the waterfront by AT&T Park, the home of the San Francisco Giants baseball team. When you walked up off Embarcadero Avenue, the main street of the waterfront, you'd see a tall white stone building. At the center of the building was a wide car path leading into a deep dark garage that seemed to go on forever. The only sign outside, hung fifteen feet off the ground, identified the building as "Pier 38: Maritime Recreational Center" and listed dock and boat rental as the primary activities inside, but there were no instructions on where to go to find them. Directly to the left and right of the car path were the only visible doors, made of rusted steel with no windows; one door had no outward-facing handle.

Many start-ups talk about being in stealth mode, but for the dozens of tech companies residing inside Pier 38, it was a literal fact. Dogpatch Labs, which hosted Instagram and Formspring, was on the first floor. Polaris Partners, True Ventures, 99designs, and dozens of other start-up and start-up-related organizations were some of the other tenants. None of these companies was particularly secretive, however; in fact, many were happy to get as much attention as possible, but the building was foreboding enough that if you didn't know exactly where you were going, you'd never find them. The entrance was more a castle gate than a red carpet. There was no security guard to ask or a directory listing to consult. Either you knew what you were doing, or you wandered around the outside of a big scary building looking like an incompetent burglar.

At the western corner of the building was a row of tall windows, each filled with an inviting column of transparent blue circles, dangling like a Calder mobile. If you made your way around the far corner, you'd see a sign that said "Automattic." Finally you'd know you were in the right place. There was no receptionist or front desk, only a glass door with a doorbell. Inside was a warm, open space with wood furniture, high ceilings, and an entire wall of inviting natural light. Bookshelves divided the loft into two sections—the one closer to the door filled with comfy couches and stylish chairs. Toward the back, a separate area had two rows of simple tables, flanked by an outrageously long bar. Rather than stocked by alcohol, it contained crates of WordPress shwag: T-shirts, caps, jackets, stickers, and buttons. The space felt like a student lounge near a fancy college library, with every decision made to inspire people into a comforting combination of studying and relaxing. There were no assigned offices or personalized spaces, not even for Schneider or Mullenweg, who both lived in San Francisco. The implication was it was a shared space, and employees could do as they wished while they were there.

The only sad thing about the office was how empty it always was. Although Automattic had eight employees living in San Francisco, the office was rarely occupied. Mostly it was used for events, meetings with the press, or big partners who expected to see a brick-and-mortar office. Whenever Mullenweg had an interview with a magazine or TV show, he'd ask all the Automatticians in the area to come in that day so the place would look legitimate. I remember the after-party for WordCamp 2009, the biggest annual WordPress conference, with the office fully alive with hundreds of people eating and dancing in every corner of the building. There was even an enormous cake with the WordPress logo, and half the partygoers had a shirt, bag, or jacket with the big W. Nöel Jackson, an Automattic designer at the time, DJed all night to a small circle of energetic dancers, watched by a much larger, and stereotypically shy, geeky crowd. Whenever I visited the office, I'd remember that vibrant night and how tame, and often lifeless, the office was now. I'd recall all the horrible cubicles I'd been in or visited and how the working masses would love to work in a place half this nice. How ironic that Automattic knew how to make it so charming yet didn't have employees interested in using it.

In late October, just before Team Social met in Greece, I flew down to San Francisco to meet with Beau, Mullenweg, and the board of directors (at Mullenweg's invitation). I'd thought of visiting earlier, but in the spirit of forcing myself to get more experience working remotely, I resisted. Mullenweg dropped hints now and then about this, and he was right. If I started a habit of flying to meet with my team, I'd never figure out alternatives. But I wondered, What about things that have no alternatives? Matt and Toni had made it clear at Seaside that their investment in paying for teams to meet was acknowledgment that some face-to-face experiences were essential. How was anyone to know what was essential and what wasn't?

I reminded myself that my primary mission was to be a great leader. I'd do my best to fit in, but I was hired to introduce different thinking, not to follow what everyone else was doing. I had to take risks and experiment, even with something as simple as how often I saw my teammates. One motivation for going to San Francisco was the recognition of how much less information you get about coworkers when you work remotely. In a conventional office, you'd know that your colleague Sally often talks to herself, or that Fred paces in the hallway when he's thinking about a tough problem. You learn their habits and how to read their body language to tell you when they're happy, sad, excited, or bored. Data about coworkers is in the air. We are social creatures, sensitive to passive data about everyone's state of mind.

Online there is no passive data. Skype and IRC let you leave a status note, and some people update them to mention their mood, but this is self-selected and filtered information. It was also text, not visual. People had avatars, but they rarely changed them. Even if they did, these were all how they chose to be seen, selected, filtered, and self-aware. I could also see what was going on in IRC, but that was activity, not passivity. If someone was having a bad day and didn't explicitly mention it in IRC, it'd be hard for me to know.

The more I tried to find out this sort of information, the more I changed what I observed. It was the Heisenberg uncertainty principle applied to remote work. If I Skyped someone to say, "How are you doing?" and he said, "Fine," and then I said, "No, really, how is everything?" even if he volunteered more, it'd be an answer I forced, different in nature from something I observed by being around them. Automatticians had to know themselves well and be outgoing online. Many were. They couldn't depend on coworkers' catching their mood or a boss recognizing something different in their behavior unless it was visible in how they expressed themselves through the narrower, text-dominant channels of remote work. Some of this might not matter or might be a boon. A coworker with body odor or who plays music too loud while working are things I was glad not to have to deal with. But good information was missing. We worked well as a team so that whatever was missed wasn't enough to give me any concerns, at least not yet.

For my San Francisco visit I scheduled time with Mullenweg, Beau, as well as Paul Kim, one of the few Automatticians with significant experience outside WordPress. He'd worked at Firefox during its rise and had reached out to me a few times in my early weeks to offer support and any advice I needed. He might have been the friendliest person in welcoming me and offering an ear. If it wasn't for Hanni and him, I doubt I'd have talked to many people I didn't work with directly at Automattic, where I didn't initiate it. There was something different in talking to people one-on-one, even in Skype, than in the group chats in IRC. I didn't initiate many of these chats myself: I often had a small worry that I was interrupting someone. Again, in a normal office, you can sense when people don't want to be interrupted. Online it's trickier. There's what their Skype status says, but that gave many fewer clues than body language does.

The realization that everyone is different when you talk to them alone is a secret to success in life. In private you have their full attention. If you talk to two children in front of their mom and then each alone, you hear different things. The mystery for why some people you know succeed or fail in life is how courageous they are in pulling people aside and how effective they are in those private conversations we never see. Only a fool thinks all decisions are made in meetings. To pitch an idea successfully is often possible only in informal, intimate situations. The same goes for speaking the deepest truths and having them heard. Almost no one can convince an entire conference room of coworkers with a speech. That happens only in the movies. Some things are never said, or heard, if more than one pair of ears is listening.

I was sure that talking to Beau would be fruitful for this reason. In the unusual world of distributed work, it's rare to talk face-to-face. It'd be an exception to have both his full attention and his eye contact at the same time. I planned to ask him for feedback on how things had gone so far and advice on what I should be doing. These were things I was sure I would have brought up informally if we worked in the same office together.

Beau grew up in a small town in rural Australia, near the southwest corner of the continent. Back in 1999 while I was working on finishing IE 5.0, he was hired for his first web job as an HTML engineer for an online insurance company. It was there he discovered and connected with PHP and MySQL, two key technologies WordPress was built with. At another company he chose WordPress as its platform and used it again for his own start-up a year later. He used the WordPress forums to get advice but soon found himself offering some too. He worked as a freelance developer for years, moving to San Francisco along the way. Happy on his own, he thought that if he were going to work for a company again, his first choice would be Automattic. On a whim, he applied on the Automattic website for a job as code wrangler, the company term for a programmer, and was disappointed not to get a reply.

A few weeks later Beau learned that Mullenweg was speaking at an MySQL meet-up (a meeting of people interested in MySQL) and saw his chance. He asked about the application, which Matt said he hadn't seen. They chatted more online, and Matt soon offered a trial project. It went well, and in May 2009 he was hired. He quickly made a name for himself with work on Gravatar and IntenseDebate, a commenting plug-in for any website that Automattic had acquired, one of the few acquisitions in company history. His favorite place to work was the center layers of code, not the deepest application programming interface or the finishing touches of the user interface. He could build anything but felt most comfortable in the middle.

If there was anything about Beau that was hard to miss, besides his 6 foot 4 inch frame and fantastic taste in music (I nominated him to be team DJ), it was his enthusiasm. He was enthusiastic about everything he did. I never did figure out if he was good at so many things because of his enthusiasm or if he enthusiastic about things because he was good at them. From studying Krav Maga, the martial art used by the Israeli army, to writing code, he took things head-on and with all his heart. He made a fantastic teammate for this reason. He was all in and ready to make things work regardless of the task, an invaluable attribute for a teammate.

We shared a long coffee across the street from the Pier at Crossroads Café, taking seats outside in the overcast October gloom of San Francisco. We talked about many things, but early on I thanked him for being first to follow my lead. New leaders need validation. It's a social challenge of being the new guy: How people who are respected treat you defines how everyone else will treat you. Beau was the first and most consistent follower of my calls for weekly meetings and posting status to P2. It was a small thing, of course. I didn't care much about status reports, but no one knew that yet. But it was one of the few visible things we shared as a team, and it mattered for that reason alone. For weeks, he was the first to respond to the status thread, which gave me a confidence boost and put pressure on Adams and Peatling to follow along. As we talked and drank coffee, and Beau clearly loved his coffee, he let me know he felt strongly that the shift to teams was good for Automattic and for him. He longed to work on bigger projects with coworkers. There were ambitious challenges he wanted to take on that could be done only if he had comrades. He was happy to do what he could to help make the transition to teams work. Independent of what he thought of me, our goals were aligned. This was great news.

Of the programmers I had, Peatling was the most self-sufficient. Prior to joining the company, he had single-handedly built a WordPress plug-in called BuddyPress, which added a social network to any WordPress site. Although there are thousands of plug-ins, most of them are small one-trick ponies that add a small feature or option WordPress didn't provide. BuddyPress was an entire system, an application layer that fundamentally changed what WordPress could do. It quickly gained in popularity because of this, and soon BuddyPress and Peatling were on Mullenweg's radar. Peatling was asked to join the company to continue working on it full time instead of as a side project.

Born in England and living at the time in Vancouver, Canada, Peatling had a glorious combination of good-natured humor and a quiet competitiveness. He had, deep in his heart, a desire to make great things. He had studied multimedia and design in college, and through a work-study program in his third year, he had his first job working on the web. He taught himself JavaScript, CSS, and PHP along the way. In the early 2000s, he had his own hand-made website and converted it to WordPress soon after it came out. He was a Renaissance man with code, combining design, user interface, and coding skills with a strong sense for the problems that users need solved. Of the Automatticians I'd met, he was the one most capable of going out on his own. Automattic hired many successful freelancers but few were product thinkers—people with visions for entire product concepts. Raanan Bar-Cohen, the lead of Team VIP Services (which handled premier clients of WordPress.com such as the BBC, CBS and UPS), often pointed this out as a cultural gap. He felt the company needed more people with entrepreneurial instincts inside the company. The fact that someone with Peatling's talents was happy to stay at Automattic said much about how much he enjoyed working there.

Mike Adams was by far the hardest for me to read. He was supportive in my first few weeks, but he was the least visible, occupied by prior projects. I also understood the least about the kinds of programming that were his strengths. Although I wasn't a programmer, I did have a computer science degree, something that, ironically, neither Adams, nor Peatling, nor Beau had. I didn't write code mostly because early in my career, I realized I did best at the level above code: leading teams, working with ideas, and shepherding projects to ship.

Over my career, I've often been asked how I could manage programmers without doing programming myself. I believe I can manage anyone making anything provided two things are true:

clarity and trust. If there is clarity between us on the goal and how we'll know when we're done, then we can speak the same language about what we need to do to get there. I knew enough about programming to call bullshit when needed and ask insightful questions. Making good things is about managing hundreds of trade-off decisions, and that's one of my best skills. Regarding clarity, most teams in the working world are starving for it. Layers of hierarchy create conflicting goals. Many teams have leaders who've never experienced clarity in their entire lives: they don't know what to look for, much less what to do when they find it. Thinking clearly, as trite as it sounds, was my strength.

Design was the ultimate provider of clarity. In situations involving technical details I didn't understand, the saving question was always, "How will this impact the user experience?" At first this sounds like a copout. Shoehorning every issue into turf I knew well could be seen as a failure to recognize my own ignorance. But with making things people will use, it's a fantastic way to understand the impact of a problem you don't understand. If a seemingly horrible bug causes only a millisecond delay for how long a blog post takes to appear, it's not horrible at all. In fact, no one but the engineer will notice it. Not being a programmer granted me a wider perspective on many issues. A smart engineer working to fix a wicked problem naturally loses perspective. Asking the user experience question is the ultimate way to prioritize engineering work, as it shifts the perspective back to where it belongs: the impact that decisions will have on customers, not engineers. Both matter, but the customer matters more.

I used similar thinking for purely technical decisions. As long as programmers and I identified the alternatives, I could ask, "What are the pros and cons of approaches A and B?" Raising the level of thinking to trade-off decisions allowed me to have valuable input on technical decisions I couldn't fix myself. Of course I was dependent on programmers to make those evaluations and define those alternatives, but that's my end of the trust equation. Provided there were clarity and trust, my lack of programming ability was an asset provided I took advantage of the perspective it offered our work.

Since Adams had the deepest understanding of WordPress's deepest code, his work was the furthest from my practical understanding. I didn't care much about what application programming interfaces we used, provided the user experience was fantastic. In the early months, I didn't have many chats with him, but he slowly became my most trusted counsel on technical matters. Beyond his programming talents, he had the preternatural ability to explain concepts at any level of abstraction. He could start describing a problem at the microscopic level, jump to ten thousand feet for a time, and then switch to anywhere in between he wished. As problem-solving partners go for a leader, his talents here were exceptional.

Leadership centers on abstractions and trade-offs: Is X faster or Y? Is A more reliable than B? Is Sally a better programmer for this than Bob? Even with design, you make bets on how the trade-offs of one direction are superior to the trade-offs of another. For many programmers, these abstractions are disturbing. The uncertainty of it is disconcerting. Much like writers and designers, they are drawn to precision work. They like the control of each pixel, bit, or letter. It satisfies perfectionistic or even obsessive compulsive tendencies in their personalities. To move to, as Adams's would say, squishy topics like choosing who to hire or fire, or what feature idea has the most merit, is distasteful for many programmers. Even programmers who are good at this often dislike it. Being a good lead is all about switching hats: knowing which level of abstraction to work at to solve a problem. It's rarely a question of intelligence; instead, it's picking the right perspective to use on a particular challenge.

Adams was a rarity: more flexible in his thinking about engineering than many vice presidents of engineering I knew and patient too. Patience is a manifestation of trust. It conveys to the other person that he or she is worth the time. It was this combination of skills and attitudes that eventually convinced me he'd make an excellent team lead. I was well ahead of myself, as my own team hadn't done much yet. But I made a note that when the opportunity arose, I needed to put him in situations where he could lead.

I returned to Seattle feeling strong. My initiation period at Automattic was over: I'd checked in with Mullenweg about my work so far, and all things were good. We talked about my plans for the team and my observations. I was ready for more experiments and to see how far my team could go.

CHAPTER 10

HOW TO START A FIRE

To understand who people really are, start a fire. When everything is going fine, you see only the safest parts of people's character. It's only when something is burning that you find out who people really are. Of course, it's wrong to set a fire on purpose, but if you have a small fire already burning, let it burn and see who, if anyone, complains, runs away, or comes to help. Similar truths are discovered by breaking rules: you need to break some to learn which are just for show and which ones matter.

In November the connector between WordPress.com and LinkedIn broke. This connector, when it worked, showed new posts on users' blogs on their LinkedIn page. This connector was one of many WordPress had with different services, including Facebook and Twitter. Thousands of posts went across these connectors every day, but the connectors were fragile. One small change in how these services accepted requests from us and our end of the connection broke. Raanan, the team lead for Team VIP Services, kindly reported the issue with a post on our P2.

This feature predated the existence of Team Social, and no one was assigned to keep it running. Urgent problems were assigned to the developer with the least on his plate, but as these issues accumulated, I worried we'd spend more time doing maintenance than new work. All services require maintenance, but when you spend more time maintaining than growing, something is wrong.

This LinkedIn issue was a good fire to learn from. What happens if we don't put it out? I thanked Raanan for the post and added it to our long list of open issues that weren't currently assigned. I'd find out how much discretion I had to decide what we fixed—or not.

Studying how a culture manages its problems is a powerful way to understand the culture. Every organization in the world has some system for it even if they don't give it a fancy name. Anthropologically speaking, the way you study this is simple. Much like how you'd tag a wild tiger with a radio collar to observe what it does in the wild, to evaluate a culture you pick an issue. Then you watch and ask:

- How and where do issues get reported?
- Who responds?
- How long does it take?
- Who decides what issues are worked on first (triage)?
- Who decides how the thing will be fixed?
- Who does the actual work?
- Who checks to make sure it was done properly?

As an example, consider the emergency room at a hospital. If a woman calls 911 to report her husband has gone into shock from overdosing on Cheetos, she'd speak to an operator who reports the issue and decides if an ambulance should be sent (or not). When Cheetos boy arrives at the hospital, the admitting nurse decides if he should be seen before or after other patients. The doctors and nurses decide on treatment, do the work (a Cheetoectomy), and assure the patient's family that he's okay. You can do a similar analysis of any workplace. It reveals who has the real power despite what the organization chart says.

For Automattic this was easy. Most of the action took place on P2s. If a customer reported an issue, Happiness handled it first. If they couldn't help, they'd post on the appropriate P2, much like Raanan did with the LinkedIn problem. If something urgent was broken, such as customers were unable to post to their websites, the issue would surface in IRC to be dealt with immediately. The bigger the issue was, the more likely it was that a more experienced person like Barry, Adams, Demitrious Kelly (another well-respected programmer), or even Mullenweg would get involved to decide how to handle it. Mostly it was up to programmers and their teams to decide how to triage issues that landed on their P2s. Some were fixed immediately, others were fixed soon, some were rejected, and others fell into the limbo of issues whose fate may never be decided.

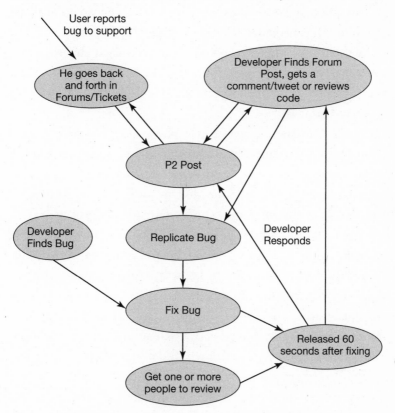

Source: Greg Brown, a code wrangler at Automattic.

If you ask the old-timers, Automattic believed in the broken window theory, the idea popularized by Jane Jacobs in her book *The Death and Life of Great American Cities.*[1] She examined why some neighborhoods in New York City were safer than others and concluded that neighborhoods that were well maintained by their inhabitants, including small things like picking up trash and fixing broken windows, tended to have less crime. In other words, by regularly fixing small things, you prevent bigger problems from starting. It's similar to the platitudes "nip it in the bud" and "an ounce of prevention is worth a pound of cure." Many open source projects espouse similar philosophies, but in practice it's a challenge since few enjoy picking up other people's trash. It was true that Adams and many other developers at Automattic would regularly watch for unowned issues to surface in IRC and jump in to debug or fix them. The broken windows theory has been challenged for not being the primary reason some neighborhoods were safer, but the premise—little things done well consistently can have big effects—has merit.

While Automattic practiced the philosophy, how far it went is another story. No matter how many Good Samaritans you have, if the rate at which windows break is faster than people can fix them, the philosophy can't save you. Most major cities have volunteers who pick up trash, but in tourist areas, it's hard to keep up with it. At least in a city, it's easy to tell how well things are going by looking around. However, looking across a large software project like WordPress.com, it was hard to know how many broken windows there are. Engineering 101 includes the concepts of incoming rates (the rate at which new problems are discovered) and fix rates (how fast they're being fixed). It's a very rough metric, but if Incoming > Fix, quality is probably going down, and if Incoming < Fix, quality is likely going up.[2] This helps project leaders understand what's going on across the project. Even hospitals and fast food restaurants use metrics like these to decide if they have enough staff or how long the average customer is going to have to wait.

But unlike many other professional software projects, WordPress.com didn't have these measures. It had a bug database, called TRAC, the same system the WordPress project itself depended on, but rarely used it. Instead each team decided on its own how to track issues on its P2s—if they tracked them at all. Few employees had worked on large software projects where these practices were common. It seemed a good idea in principle to adopt something better, but as chaotic as Automattic was, quality seemed to be okay. WordPress, and WordPress.com, didn't yet have a reputation for being buggy or unreliable. Changing to a different system would challenge the culture, and without a specific problem to justify the change, I didn't see the point in trying. I tried to remember Mullenweg's attitude of letting that which did not matter, not matter. Maybe with the right culture and talent, you didn't need some of the fundamental things experts claim you need. Start-up companies get away with it all the time, but WordPress.com was not a start-up anymore.

On Team Social we tracked issues in the simplest way possible: we made lists. As programmers fixed them, we crossed them off. It was easy to see how many were fixed and how many were left, or to add comments to a particular issue. Where it failed was triage: all bugs tended to be treated equally. Important issues, trivial issues, challenging bugs, and easy fixes were all listed in the same way. The common designations of priority (Is this priority 1, 2 or 3?) and severity (Are we deleting customers' blog posts, or did we just misspell something?) didn't exist. Everyone used their own judgment to decide what was important. We talked as a team about the dangers of this, and for specific projects, I led triage and made the first lists, putting things in priority order. I'd also catch any issues no one else had picked up that I thought were important and ask a specific programmer to investigate. It was ad hoc, but I made sure triage was part of the process.

I wasn't alone in thinking that the company needed a better system. Every few months, a debate would rise on Updates, the company watercooler P2. Someone would advocate a shift to using TRAC heavily, with all issues logged and tracked in its database. The pro-TRAC faction was often led by Peter Westwood, a long-time WordPress contributor and a programmer on Team Happiness. That team spent the most time managing bugs. and it was no surprise they'd be the strongest advocates for a better process. But sweeping change was hard to come by. Each team was free to do as it wished, and few used TRAC. Team Social would eventually be one of the first to try switching, but not until months later.

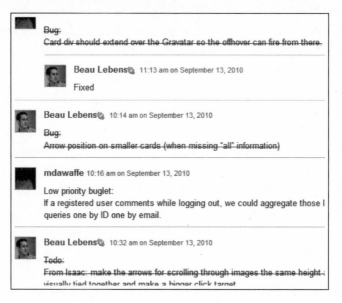

Each team developed its own process variations. Although they never used the P word (*process*), a word that smelled of big corporations, that's what it was. One team improved P2 itself to allow posts to be marked as unresolved, making filtering possible. Often programmers would cherry-pick bugs they felt were most important or easiest to do, and leave the others alone—a kind of modified broken window theory where people pick the windows they like most or are closest to their homes. Team Social, like other teams, designated the lead to be the last line of defense, responding to unanswered P2 posts.

The broken LinkedIn connector itself wasn't important. Not many people used it—maybe 1 percent of all users. Raanan was one of the few at Automattic who did, and he reported the problem first because he saw it first. No one else on Team Social noticed. This sounds like a breach of ethics because we were the team responsible for it. The challenge, however, was that there were more features to support than our team could use personally. I considered making a simple testing table, dividing up all the things we were responsible for and assigning someone on the team to periodically check them, but it never happened. Instead we relied on the Happiness team, Twitter, Facebook, and our users to be our early warning system. Our quality control measures were responsive, not proactive. New features were handled differently, but for systems already working, we assumed we'd hear about it if something went wrong.

A few days later, another person reported the LinkedIn issue. Finally Mullenweg reported it too. The volume of reports increased, ending my fire experiment. I asked Beau to take a look and sort it out. The lesson wasn't surprising: mostly what I learned was that I wanted a better way to prioritize defects. Depending on anecdotal reports from users was a poor system. It'd be like running a restaurant where you waited for customers to complain about the food instead of tasting it ourselves before it left the kitchen. But I stayed patient. I floated my observations now and then, but I'd wait until someone felt enough frustration to pursue a change, at least in my first few months. Only then would I have a partner in trying out a solution. And more important perhaps, only then would changing how we work be warranted. If my frustrations weren't matched by the frustrations of the people doing the work, perhaps it was my problem and not theirs.

There's an old joke about how IBM, the leading software company in the 1970s, tried to measure productivity among its workers.[3] Executives wanted a way to measure how complex projects were, and after consideration, they decided to track lines of programming code. The theory was that longer programs were better, or harder to make, than shorter ones, which implied that better programmers wrote more lines of code. From an assembly line perspective, this was a decent theory: a person who can make twenty bricks in an hour is better than one who makes only five. The mistake was assuming that programming (and most other creative work) is a volume task, which it isn't. Better programmers needed fewer lines of code in their projects when they are finished, not more. Only someone unfamiliar with the attributes of good programming work could invent such a backward measurement.

Today many managers love the saying, "You are what you measure." They're convinced measurement is the secret to success and seek metrics to track—sometimes called KPIs, or key performance indicators, much like IBM executives did back then. Some companies, including Google, insist on having metrics to evaluate any decision, goal, or feature. Despite the popularity of this belief, it's easy to get lost in the very metrics that are supposed to help you find your way.

The trap is that even if you find a good metric that avoids the trap IBM fell into, people will naturally, even subconsciously, work to game the metric. They want to "do good," and once leaders put up a scoreboard that everyone sees, it has unexpected power. Workers can't resist hourly glances at the score, reinforcing gentle nudges in how they make decisions that juke the number upward, at the cost of everything else that isn't represented on the scoreboard. Want to increase new sign-ups for your service? Fine. It's easy to get more sign-ups if you don't care if "customers" never return or you don't have a good filter against spam.

Eventually everyone realizes that the metric, which was good for a time, is now being gamed. Employees go so far out of their way to score well on the metric that it has negative effects on the real quality of what the company makes, something people recognize intuitively. And as is the way of things, the number-centric leader who created the original KPI decides the solution is to create more, and more precise, KPIs. More are added, which might help at first, but soon the same pattern repeats and the problem is amplified. You see a similar downward spiral at schools that try to measure teacher performance. They create new student tests for evaluating teachers that reduce time teachers have to teach real lessons, which lowers their scores, which, sad surprise, leads to more testing.

All metrics create temptations. Even with great intentions and smart minds, data runs you faster and faster into a stupid self-destructive circle. Data can't decide things for you. It can help you see things more clearly if captured carefully, but that's not the same as deciding. Just as there is an advice paradox, there is a **data paradox:** no matter how much data you have, you still depend on your intuition for deciding how to interpret and then apply the data.

Put another way, there is no good KPI for measuring KPIs. There are no good metrics for evaluating metrics (or for evaluating metrics for evaluating metrics for evaluating metrics, and on it goes). When a culture shifts too far into faith in data, people with great intuitions leave. They'll find employment where their judgment is valued rather than remain as an annoyance in some powerful equation maker's report. Making great things requires both intuition and logic, not a dominance of one over the other. Beauty, inspiration, and pleasure are qualities that corporations hope customers find in their products, yet none are easily measured. If you want to explain the difference between Apple, BMW, and IKEA and Microsoft, Fiat, and Walmart, KPIs alone will not help you.

Automattic is fascinating for its complex relationship with data. Whereas tracking bugs holds little interest, there is a sophisticated reporting system for data about what's happening live on WordPress.com. Called MC, or MissionControl, it lets employees answer questions about what users are doing. Want to know how many posts were published this hour? How many comments? How many new blogs were created? What themes they chose? How many millions of people visited last week and what countries they were from? It's all there. You can make charts and comparisons to answer thousands of questions, including queries that compare data from different years, months, or days of the week. Access to this information is a godsend for designers. They don't have to imagine what happens: they can see a representation of what people do or have done. For anyone who has never worked on a live service, MC is a dream: many stupid debates about user behavior go away. Of course, explaining why customers behave as they do is another, and far more difficult question. It was easy to spend hours playing with MC. Sometimes seeing a graph of data for something you think you know reveals surprises. One day while I was investigating a theory on which WordPress.com blogs had the most traffic, I found a chart of all the traffic, reported in daily increments. The chart had a strange scalloped pattern, making a consistently wavy line. It took me a few minutes to figure out what it was: weekends. Traffic on most websites drops on Saturday and Sunday, explaining the odd rhythm to the chart.

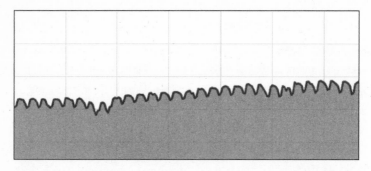

When I was hired, I paid attention to how Mullenweg commented on discussions on various P2s. He frequently linked to charts and tables relevant to the discussion. Although he was not using these as a hammer to end arguments, he regularly referred to data as part of his thinking. He wanted a data-influenced culture, not a data-driven one. He didn't make data the center of the conversation but wanted to ensure they were part of it. His balance of respect for both intuition and analysis was one of his most notable qualities. I could tell who had been at the company longer because they were the ones more likely to refer to statistics in their posts, even if they had doubts about what exactly they meant. (Often there were multiple sources of data that could be used to answer a question and they'd offer different answers, further support for the data paradox.) This would be frustrating if you had faith that data could decide things for you, but useful if your goal instead was simply to shed more light on what was going on to make more informed decisions.

Data was recorded about employees too, and not just their Happiness statistics. Since P2s were visible to all, MC recorded basic information about everyone's activity. Team Social's averaged eight posts or comments per day, the second most active in the company. Updates P2, the company watercooler, averaged nearly fifteen. You could find similar reports per P2, per employee, broken down by posts, comments, and other details. Much like data about users, data about employees was never used to judge people. The general advice you'd hear is that everyone should be active and communicate, but there were no quotas. It was a scoreboard, but one you had to go out of your way to find, much like my experience during my support tour. There was a mature balance of reporting data yet leaving people free to decide what they meant or how much they wanted to use in their thinking. MC was a manifestation of the line between support and creatives. MC was a tool, created by the Janitorial team, to support all the others in doing their work. But rarely would the data dictate to anyone what should be done.

CHAPTER 11

REAL ARTISTS SHIP

In September 1983, the Apple Macintosh project was far behind schedule. The team was burning out but still had significant work left to do. Steve Jobs, CEO of Apple and visionary leader of the project, walked by the team's main hallway and wrote on a nearby easel what would become one of his best-known sayings: "Real Artists Ship." He wrote it because he wanted to compel the project team to work harder and finish sooner. Today the quote is used as a rallying cry for creatives in many professions—people who overlook how at the time Jobs was emphasizing shipping, not artistry. Merely shipping something does not make you an artist. However, the only way the world learns of what makers makes, whether it's art or trash, is when they're brave enough to say it's done and put it out into the world.

Jobs's quote makes it easy to forget that no one starts a project planning *not* to ship. It's not as if entire divisions of smart, hard-working people toil away for months with a deep and passionate hope that when they're finished, their work will be boxed up in wooden crates and shipped to the warehouse from *Indiana Jones and the Raiders of The Lost Ark*, never to be seen again. Everyone who passionately makes things is driven by a desire to see what they make in use by whomever they made it for. If anything, most people with big ideas think too soon about shipping, spending their first epiphany-fueled evenings dreaming of the glory the world will bestow on them after they've shipped, despite the fact they have yet to do any of the work. Dreams are free; shipping must be earned.

Shipping anything can be difficult, even if it's just a college term paper or a Thanksgiving dinner. Right now thousands of entrepreneurs and programmers are spinning their wheels, either stuck on seemingly unsolvable problems or obsessing on details few customer will notice. There are many cunning traps in trying to ship, which explains why many people get lost in the limbo between starting and finishing. Making things is hard regardless of your philosophy or what adage you frame on your wall. Most projects run over schedule or over budget, or they get cancelled. When you look around at all the machines, books, gadgets, and applications in our lives, it's amazing they were finished at all.

At the heart of the debate over how to overcome the challenges of shipping good things is an idea referenced in the title of Eric Raymond's book *The Cathedral and the Bazaar*.[1] The book, which is about observations on making software, raises a central question that is relevant to all work: Is it better to invest time in making a big masterful plan or instead to start immediately and figure it out as you go?

If you imagine the architect of a towering skyscraper or the director of a big-budget motion picture, you probably envision a singular brilliant tyrant who has detailed plans for how everything will be done. This is *cathedral*-style thinking. The town of Seaside, from chapter 6, based on a single master plan, embodied this approach. For the alternative, imagine a young punk rock band jamming together. They start with something small, a few basic chords, but quickly revise it, and revise it again, each contributing, borrowing, experimenting, and collaborating as they wish. This is the *bazaar*. Instead of grand central planning, a community of work forms around an idea and grows. Many famous open source projects, such as the Linux operating system, were developed using bazaar attitudes, and this inspired Raymond's book. However, most of the rest of the world, including most of the software industry, believes in the cathedral. (In practice, it's a false dichotomy: most things are made with a combination of cathedral and bazaar approaches, though the balance varies greatly.) Unlike skyscrapers, digital works lend themselves to the incremental changes that come easily with bazaar attitudes. Software rarely has the same risks that airplanes, bridges, or even soufflés have, where one mistake can ruin the whole thing. Whereas most software is unregulated, bridges, medical equipment, and automobiles have safety standards that must be verified before a product can launch, motivating the rigor those professions use. The fear of big mistakes or falling behind schedule is what motivated most of the project management processes used around the world. The more experienced that managers are, the longer the list of bad things they've seen that they're trying to avoid. This is what I call *defensive management*, since it's designed to prevent a long list of bad things from happening. Defensive management is blind to recognizing how obsessing about preventing bad things also prevents good things from happening or sometimes even prevents anything from happening at all.

At WordPress.com something shipped every day. Often it was something small like a bug fix or minor improvement, but it was new nevertheless. By the time I was hired in August 2010, there had been twenty-five thousand releases of WordPress.com, and there would be over fifty thousand by the time I left in 2012. Toni Schneider used the term *continuous deployment* to describe the philosophy of endless small changes.[2] Everyone who visited a website hosted on WordPress.com would always be using the latest version, possibly only seconds old. Programmers and designers could ship as often as they wished, which generally meant as soon as they finished. There was no testing queue or review board. No schedules or master plans were needed, since there was no need for deadlines, dates, or other coordination. There was little management since there was little to defend against. In the worst case—perhaps a release accidentally replaced all blogs with blinking images of zombie bananas—it could be reverted, restoring the software to how it was before. But reverting code was rare. Instead programmers were encouraged to make another change that fixed the problem. As a rule, everyone who launched something was expected to stay online for a few hours to ensure things went smoothly.

The absence of a grand schedule removed the constant fear of falling behind that many projects create and replaced it with small but frequent payoffs that we were making things better. Work felt more like a meal of Spanish tapas, with small plates of deliciousness arriving every few minutes. You didn't have to wait in line or for the next mealtime. Customers didn't have to wait either: they'd always be using the latest version no matter what they were doing. Any employee could watch in IRC as new improvements, or patches as they were often called, were shared between programmers to help test them before they went live.

Sometimes as many as twenty-five changes would go live on a single day. On busy days, IRC would be filled with programmers coordinating their launches, making sure no collisions occurred, and it was always fun to watch. By comparison, back when I worked on Microsoft Windows in the 1990s, we released a new version every few years. When I worked on Internet Explorer during the browser wars of the 1990s, we shipped at most every month. Working in the chaos of WordPress.com was something many of my friends thought would be hard for me to do, given all of the big project experience I had.

It turned out the adjustment was easy. The Internet Explorer team at Microsoft had an equivalent, called the *daily build*, where we released a version of the software every day, but it was available exclusively inside the company.[3] Each day all the changes from the previous day were compiled and released, and everyone was expected to install and use them. This gave us regular feedback on the quality of what we were making, including nuggets of joy, or moments of misery, when new features were added. On good days, the builds were high quality, and we called those releases *self-host*, as in "safe to host on your computer." Builds that were mediocre were called *self-test*, suggesting you install it only on a test computer (or a coworker's when the person wasn't looking). The worst builds were called *self-toast*, meaning you'd destroy whatever machine you had dared installed it on. Whenever we had three days in a row with self-toast builds, all new work stopped until we got the build quality up to a good level (a measure to prevent the project from digging a dangerously deep quality hole for itself). Shipping on WordPress.com was the same philosophy, just accelerated and made public to customers. I didn't find the lack of bigger plans or schedules a problem. In fact, it was mostly liberating.

To anyone who has worked on a large project, this all sounds like madness. How can they work without schedules? How can there be no safeguards? Why wouldn't things blow up and collide all the time? A major reason it works at Automattic is belief in a counterintuitive philosophy: *safeguards don't make you safe; they make you lazy*. People drive faster, not more slowly, in cars with antilock brakes. American football players take more risks, not fewer, because of their padding. At Automattic, the traps of trying to make things safe are resisted, although people are motivated more by their sense of independence than an awareness of a grand philosophical principle. The basic notion is that if people are smart and respect not blowing things up, too many safety measures get in the way. Instead, employees are trusted and empowered to release things fast.

The idea that safety measures make you unsafe reminded me of a trip I took to Delhi, India, years ago. I climbed to the top of a stone tower at Jantar Mantar, an amazing public park of gigantic astronomical instruments. Four stories off the ground, one building curved sharply upward on a tricky and narrow staircase, with no railings. A fall would kill anyone. I climbed with much greater care than if there had been a railing. Small children and old men climbed with me, all of us stepping gingerly along the way, our built-in sense of danger doing more than enough to keep us safe. A similar attitude was at work at WordPress.com. Employees were treated like adults. By not having too many safeguards, we were trusted to pay full attention. Keeping things a little dangerous made things safer.

But safety wasn't my biggest concern. It wasn't creativity either, as there were lists of ideas everywhere, not including the thousands of plug-ins and themes WordPress had, each with inspirations for new possibilities for how to make WordPress.com better. The problem was coherence. We certainly launched many things, but did it add up to making a better product?

Despite all the joy WordPress folks took in making fun of Microsoft and other old-school software companies, Word-Press's user interface was complicated. It felt more like something Microsoft would make than Apple, despite the company's great fondness for Apple products. Historically Mullenweg was the primary source for product vision at Automattic, and in most ways he was still the visible leader in the open source WordPress project too. He was talented at thinking about design. But as WordPress and WordPress.com had gotten bigger, there was less of him to go around and a growing pile of legacy features and options to wrestle with. What started as a simple, streamlined tool with .71 now had hundreds of features, all competing for attention from users, the classic consequence of continuous deployment. Each programmer over the years had thought only about his or her own little idea, and not how it competed with the hundreds of other ideas already in the product.

I'd seen this before. The solution is vision. Someone has to define what we're trying to get to and clarify which ideas are both more and less important in completing that vision. To simplify a design requires thinking holistically—how the whole thing fits together for the user—rather than how good any idea seems on its own. For all of the strengths of WordPress's bazaar culture, its user experience lacked the grace and clarity a cathedral architect would naturally provide.

On Team Social's P2, I described one simple vision. Without mentioning a single feature idea, I described the most important steps all customers go through:

Get Idea → Write it → Publish → Be happy

This seems simple, and it is. WordPress is not a spreadsheet program or a 3D modeling tool; it's a machine for putting things online. If you look at WordPress's Post screen, the one place people spend more time than any other, most of it is taken up by a big edit box that anyone instantly recognizes as a word processor. And then in the upper right is a big blue button that says PUBLISH. What could be simpler?

But the problem isn't functionality. Functionality means a piece of software is capable of doing something. Merely having a function doesn't say anything about how many people can figure it out or are even interested in trying. Your car might be equipped with dual warp drives, but if you can't find it or figure out how to use it, what good is the ability to travel at the speed of light? Not good at all. It's design, not functionality, that determines if people will succeed or fail in fulfilling the promises products have made to them.

And as anyone who has tried to write knows, blank pages are intimidating. Even for people who have many ideas, having the idea in your mind is one thing, but putting it down into paragraphs worthy of publishing is another. WordPress users had their own dilemma around shipping. Instead of "Real Artists Ship," the corollary for bloggers should probably be "Real Bloggers Publish." The problem was that WordPress did little to help users with this first and significant challenge.

After more thought, I realized many bloggers create blogs but give up before they even publish a single post. For many, the sequence is this:

Get Blog → Abandon

or

$$\text{Get Blog} \rightarrow \text{Get Idea} \rightarrow \text{Abandon}$$

A percentage of users do better: they get at least as far as putting a draft together but go no further:

$$\text{Get idea} \rightarrow \text{Draft a Post} \rightarrow \text{Abandon}$$

Of those who draft a post, a fraction manage to do a second draft but then give up:

$$\text{Get idea} \rightarrow \text{Draft a Post} \rightarrow \text{Edit/Revise} \rightarrow \text{Abandon}$$

And in the best possible case, when the user makes it all the way and actually hits Publish, there are two possible outcomes. The one everyone hopes for looks like this:

$$\text{Get idea} \rightarrow \text{Draft a Post} \rightarrow \text{Edit/Revise} \rightarrow$$
$$\text{Publish} \rightarrow \text{Get love and attention}$$

But the more common one is probably:

$$\text{Get idea} \rightarrow \text{Draft a Post} \rightarrow \text{Edit/Revise} \rightarrow$$
$$\text{Publish} \rightarrow \text{Get silence}$$

When you look at WordPress this way, it's a tough road. Even for people who manage to make it past all of the hurdles where most people give up, they are met with an uncaring, silent universe when they finally publish. WordPress barely indicated anything good happened at all, offering a tiny, terse sentence that said "post published" at the top of the screen. I'm sure some users wonder if they'd done something wrong given our perfunctory confirmation of their hours of work. And if it's their first post on a new blog, it's guaranteed there will be no traffic, and without traffic, there are no comments from visitors. It's an anticlimactic experience. The additional challenge of getting attention online for a blog required weeks of effort, a challenge we did little to help users understand or overcome.[4]

The lesson for Automattic was: features weren't the problem. We had plenty of features and compared favorably with competitors. Adding more features would have little impact on moving more people through the sequence of publishing unless those features helped users get over the first hurdles, and few did. I asked Martin Remy, the lead of Team Data, to give us statistics on the hypothesis I had. Team Data had many jobs, including building one of the most popular features on WordPress.com: the statistics module that told bloggers exactly how many page views they had every day. One of their other roles was to help teams like mine answer questions with information about what users were doing. The numbers were staggering: more than 50 percent of all blogs never publish a single post. That high number reflected two problems.

First, low use rates are common for free web services. Most of the popular ones like Twitter, Facebook, and Gmail are proud to tell you how many "users" they have but conveniently skip past the low statistics for how many of those "users" have ever been active at all or had even logged in once during the past month. Second, many people are told by their friends, "You should have a blog." They create a blog on WordPress.com in seconds, but this turns out to be easier than writing a post. Many people create blogs without specific plans or a sense of what to expect in the first month. Much like buying a guitar with hopes of learning to play, merely owning a guitar, or a blog, doesn't come with the commitment to use it.

By framing the problem around my simple scenario, we had a way to evaluate the merit of specific feature ideas:

- Will this feature get more people further along in the scenario?
- Will this get them more rewards when they publish?

We decided feature ideas that address these goals were more important than all others.

One idea that fit well was to notify a blogger with an e-mail every time someone responded to something on their blog. Although we had provided visitors many ways to indicate they liked something they read, including a feature similar to Facebook's Like button, we did nothing to inform the blogger that it happened. Our goal thus became to send simple e-mails to the blogger when some of these good news events happened. It was far from a genius idea, but we didn't need genius; we simply needed to build features that helped our customers in the most important way.

I wrote up the launch announcement and asked Peatling, who had built the Like feature itself, to work on the notification functionality. Beau and Adams helped out with some of the technical plumbing needed and built an additional e-mail for subscriptions (meaning that if a visitor subscribed to the blog, we'd e-mail the blogger with the good news). The work took only a couple of days since we could reuse code for other e-mails that WordPress.com was already sending to users. We picked a few data points to track, including how many people disabled the notifications (each e-mail included instructions for how to do it). We wanted to know if this feature was more annoying that useful.

We always planned to be online together for feature launches, a good safety measure in case things went wrong and we needed to respond quickly. But it was also emotionally satisfying to release something new into the world together. There was always lots of joking around on Team Social. In the prelaunch countdown, which we ran in similar fashion to NASA launches, we'd always find small issues we had missed that required only one person to fix, leaving the rest of us to entertain each other. Often I made a teamwide bet about one of the data points we were going to collect to help keep us interested. We agreed on this particular day to launch at 12:30, but actually launched at 12:44 PST. Here's the IRC transcript:

12:44: *berkun:* bets on when we see our first disable?
12:44: *mdawaffe:* 12:52 PST
12:45: *berkun:* wait—what's the bet?:)
12:45: *mdawaffe:* umm ... I don't know
12:45: *apeatling:* first round next meetup
12:45: *apeatling:* round of beers that is

12:45: *mdawaffe:* sounds reasonable

12:46: *apeatling:* wait, that means you buy for winning, that doesn't seem right:)

12:46: *mdawaffe:* oh—haha

12:46: *beaulebens:* no, if you win, everyone else buys you a drink:)

12:46: *mdawaffe:* are those 3 enables just us testing?

12:47: *beaulebens:* that's the one

12:47: *apeatling:* I'm calling:51

12:47: *mdawaffe:* ha

12:47: *beaulebens:* I say:58

12:48: *berkun:* I'll go long and say 1:15

12:48: *beaulebens:* is this for subscriptions or likes disable? Or either?

12:48: *berkun:* either

12:51: *mdawaffe:* ok peatling, you're minutes on

12:51: *beaulebens: hits refresh again and again and again*

12:51: *apeatling:* come on haters!

12:51: *beaulebens:* apeatling no disabling it yourself

12:51: *apeatling:* haha

15:51: *berkun:* haha

Two days after launch, we had rich data showing the trends for how often each notification was sent out. We soon learned that eighteen thousand notifications were sent each day, about half for Likes and half for subscriptions. The number of users who turned the feature off was very low, a good sign.

For every feature Team Social launched, we used the same process. Often after launch we'd discover new bugs or recognize patterns in the data that didn't make sense, which we'd investigate. Sometimes we'd redesign parts of the feature in response and repeat the process on a much smaller scale. After forty-eight hours of responding to launch issues, things quieted down and we'd move on. Sometimes we'd decide to do another round of work on the same feature or move on to new ones.

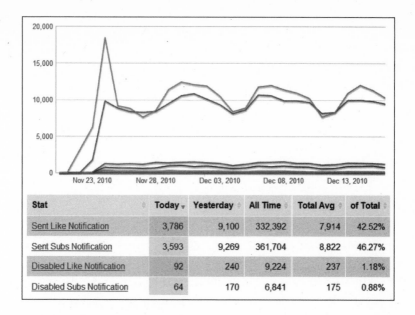

Stat	Today ▼	Yesterday	All Time	Total Avg	of Total
Sent Like Notification	3,786	9,100	332,392	7,914	42.52%
Sent Subs Notification	3,593	9,269	361,704	8,822	46.27%
Disabled Like Notification	92	240	9,224	237	1.18%
Disabled Subs Notification	64	170	6,841	175	0.88%

More than anything else, working in this fashion was fun. We were a small team, we worked fast, we had all the data we could ask for to help us make decisions, and we liked working together. The challenge I had was how to make meaning of what we did. Anyone could make small features and launch them. We needed to make bigger bets beyond just features, and they had to be features aimed in the right direction.

After three months of working together, we planned our first meet-up for Athens, Greece. It'd be there that the two big bets for the rest of my tenure as Team Social's lead would be made.

CHAPTER 12

ATHENS LOST AND FOUND

In the middle of a sea of traffic in Athens, my taxi driver told me to get out of the car. It was November 2010, and the Greek debt crisis was rippling through the country. Union protesters, in an angry effort to compel Greece's parliament not to take away their pay, had closed the downtown core of the city. My driver took me deep into the fray, but the main boulevard into the downtown quarter was blocked off, guarded by city police. When he pointed and cursed at the traffic, saying I needed to get out, I didn't understand. I thought he was being sarcastic. "Yeah right," I said, joking in response. Having a cab driver merely point and curse at the landscape of traffic horrors on the other side of the windshield lends itself to many interpretations. Sensing my confusion, he explained again and apologized, offering in clear English that he could go no farther. From the well-practiced shrug of his shoulders, I sensed this was an apology he'd offered many times lately. He told me I could take the subway train the rest of the way and wrote the name of the stop I needed on the back of a receipt. There was a station a few blocks away, and he showed me which train to take. I paid him, grabbed my bags, and headed up the street, bewildered but also excited. The luxury of taking a taxi is not having to think, but a taxi is a mobile ivory tower. The strike forced me out into the open for better and for worse.

Unable to read Greek, I unsurprisingly failed to find my train. There were plenty of signs and arrows above the pathways in and out of the main part of the station, but their meaning was beyond the cognition of a foreigner fresh off an airplane. The note from the taxi driver was illegible enough you'd have rights to believe it was any one of a half-dozen languages. After standing far too long as a helpless fool looking down at my note and up at the signs, I gave up. With no other choice, I took my last option: I pleaded my case with a very unfriendly woman behind the ticket counter.

Her lack of grace was not surprising. No one loves ticket counter work. There is no child in school dreaming of counting coins to make change or telling cranky foreigners, day after day, where to find the same damn bathroom. Yet because of my support tour at Automattic, I saw customer service differently than I had in the past, and waiting in line gave me time to consider the comparisons. Her job was to help people use the transportation system, just as happiness engineers helped people use a publishing system. What if her job were designed the same way as those of happiness engineers are? Working in a train station, a physical place, meant she had to work in person and with set hours, but otherwise why couldn't some of the happiness engineer model be applied? At their core, both jobs were about teaching people to do something the system is supposed to let them do.

One major difference that might explain her unfriendliness was the organizational philosophy. The Athens Transportation Authority (ATA) had, I assumed, a cathedral style of management. This woman had no control over how she worked, when she worked, or, most important, how she provided help to customers. It was obvious that someone at cathedral planning HQ, miles away, had designed all the signs with the arrows. Architects are notorious for designing and disappearing, never returning to see how their choices worked or failed after the building opens. Instead of their treating this woman like a robot, what if she had power to make smart changes, even just small ones? Why couldn't she be empowered to learn from the questions she heard every day and try to find ways to improve the signs or the pamphlets so more people found their way without her help? If, like Automattic, every new executive at the ATA had to work on the front lines for three weeks, how would the job of ticket clerk be redefined and empowered? Wouldn't that be in everyone's interest, from the clerk, to the executive, to the customer? The line moved at a crawl, largely due to this woman's lack of intrinsic or extrinsic motivation, granting me plenty of reflection time.

Automattic hired people for their love of WordPress, begging the question whether this woman, or any of her coworkers, had any interest in trains at all. Of course, Greece could barely afford to pay anyone, and perhaps all of Greece's friendly trainophiles had migrated elsewhere. A philosophy can't do much if you can't pay people what they're worth. But then again, WordPress was fueled by volunteers working on their own time. Could something like WordPress's culture work for government? Or for a public service? I didn't know. In the end, I got what I needed from the woman behind the counter, but nothing more. Without once hinting she understood a word of my English, she waited for me to finish talking, lifted a limp finger, and pointed it in the direction of the train I needed. I was on my way and soon arrived at the hotel and settled in.

While we'd worked online for weeks and had met at Seaside, the team hadn't spent much time together in person. It's new territory to travel with someone, and as a group we still had much to figure out about how to get along together in person. When Beau, Peatling, Adams, and I met in the lobby just after dark, we first had to sort out what to do. Team-specific meet-ups were new, and we were one of the first teams to do one. We eventually decided to wander out for a meal, but our wandering did not go well. Despite the massive computing power of our smart phones and general street savvy of our group, our travel fatigue led to the mistake known as the walk of indifference. We strolled past various restaurants stopping to glance at menus or peeking inside, but were just indifferent enough about everything we saw to keep wandering on.

The first night in a city has conflicting urges: one to relax and get settled after a long day of travel, the other to see the city and experience something special. No one wants to end up at the Hard Rock Café in a hotel lobby, but following the temptation to seek an ideal dining experience with three other jet-lagged people who had never traveled together before was a mistake. Ambiguity makes everyone tolerant of incompetence.

For reasons none of us can explain, we ended up as the lone patrons at the saddest and most downtrodden-looking restaurant we'd seen. On the dark edge of a brightly lit stretch of tourist traps, we took an outdoor table at an indoor restaurant, an establishment, we'd learn later, was staffed by a sole employee. Mostly he smoked cigarettes or disappeared in the downstairs kitchen for ten minutes at a time. The only memorable moment of an otherwise entirely forgettable meal was a young homeless girl, maybe eleven years old, who begged for money at our table. With no one else around, we were easy to spot as tourists, and with no protection from our restaurant staff, she just stood next to our table saying, "Please . . . please," again and again. Her sweet brown eyes and long dark hair looked healthy enough, and she was clothed well, but perhaps a long day of begging so many weeks after the tourist season ended hadn't proved fruitful. "Please . . . please," she said staring into our eyes. She put out her hand over the edge of our table. We hadn't received any food yet, which we assumed meant she wanted only money.

In the first moment, it was moving: a hungry child asking for help. It played on the most basic instincts of compassion we all have. "Please . . . please," she repeated, making eye contact with each of us for long moments. But her tone was more a demand than a request, making it harder to connect with her. For reasons

I can't explain, it seemed a mistake to contribute. Her aggressive persistence made the situation confrontational. After several long, agonizing minutes, she left. It was disturbing and sad. I still feel regret and wonder what we should have done. I do sometimes give food to people on the street, but her aggression shut down those instincts. (After the trip, I donated to The Smile of the Child, a Greek charity that looks after homeless children.[1])

The reason I share this story is that the shock of the experience woke us out of our collective jet-lagged stupor. It was strange for all us, and as uncomfortable as we were, we'd shared what had just happened. The intensity of that memory, even now, is beyond anything our team could ever have experienced online. Although we gave her nothing, she gave us the gift of a story to share—something a new team on their first adventure together needed to find. The encounter woke all of us up.

After we ate, knowing Mullenweg would arrive later that night, we looked for a pub nearby to wait and combat our jet lag. By sheer luck, we found a small bar just around the corner from our hotel. Dimly lit and without a proper sign out front, the Plaka Café was hard to recognize as a place of business. It could as easily have been the first-floor living room of a bohemian neighbor. A few empty tables sat outside the door, and an older couple sat on stools inside and near the back. Otherwise it was empty and quiet. The liveliest patron was at the bar, chatting with the barkeep, who, we guessed, was also the owner. Hoping for a quiet place to chat that could also serve us food and beer, we noticed the balcony upstairs and thought we might have found a winner. We asked if it was okay to use the balcony (it could have been part of a residence and not the café) and got an enthusiastic yes. We saw beer on tap and some snacks and knew we'd found a home.

The narrow, twisting wooden staircase led to a balcony that epitomized a freshman college dorm. Beneath a low ceiling was a set of backless seats with colorful yellow pillows, ancient lamps, deep orange walls, and floral light fixtures tucked in below the ceiling. A mostly empty bookcase stood in a corner, and oddly sized pictures were framed on some of the walls. Soon, rounds of Mythos, the local beer that only foreigners drink, were in our hands and our energy returned. Our friendly but nameless barkeep brought a small bowl of spiced potato chips with each round, a small touch that to our weary travelers' eyes seemed a glorious innovation. A lively conversation arose, and we rallied our way deep into a glorious combination of Mythos, jokes, and fun debates about what our team should be working on.

When Mullenweg finally arrived, we'd had a fair share of Mythos, and our spirits were high. As Matt rounded the top step of the balcony, Adams stood up, ran over to him, and hugged him. But then the Mythos took hold, and they toppled over together. As they fell toward the wall, we let out a collective gasp, fearing it would be our teammate who killed our fearless leader. They barely missed the huge picture frame on the wall and crashed hard on the floor. When their survival was certain, we laughed and, to ensure a proper toast for Mullenweg's arrival, ordered another round. With spirits high, time flew by, and soon the balcony bar was closing down. We'd been the only people in the place for hours, and at 2:00 a.m. the owner's hospitality reached its end. He told us the only other bar likely to be open that late was called Jokers, just a few blocks away.

As we rambled through the narrow cobbled streets, we discovered the sidewalks were protected from cars by rows of posts called bollards, each three feet high and nearly four feet apart. Among other juvenile dares and challenges we made of each other on that walk, Beau bet he could jump from the top of one bollard to another. As all friends do, we cheered him on. As engineers, we briefly discussed his odds, evaluating the surface area of the domed posts, considerations for the optimal angle and height of the jump, and even how much the uneven alignment of the posts might factor in. Ending the speculation, Beau quickly rose up on the nearest post like the Karate Kid, one foot forward, arms out, and then crouched down to leap.

He made it to the next post, impressive on its own, and leaped to the third. Midair, his trajectory seemed wrong, raising the question of what the correct trajectory would have to have been. His foot rolled off the top of the post, and he fell hard toward the pavement, arms out and only cement below. But as was typical for Beau, either through Australian training for drunk jumping or a special Krav Maga technique he'd learned, midfall he realized his predicament and managed to tuck and roll, landing in the street on his back in a rolling motion, hitting only his elbow on the ground. He stood up, clearly surprised that the capacity for standing was still available to him and, with great excitement to still be alive, checked himself for wounds. The silver-dollar-sized patch of skin missing from his elbow seemed a fair price to pay, and he was glad. And so were we. Still rallying, we stumbled onward to the Joker, a tiny bar consisting primarily of a crowded stairwell. We set ourselves up on a table outside, talking and drinking almost until the sun rose. With the din of the bar behind us, we shared a beautiful night as new friends on the silent streets of Athens.

Late in the morning, we met for a long breakfast outside. I had clear ideas for how the meet-up should go, and with the first night out of the way, I wanted work to begin. However, with Mullenweg there, it seemed best to follow his lead about what form that work should take. As rare as it was to work in person, team chats with Matt were rarer, and that deserved priority. In the beautiful outdoor garden behind our hotel, with views of the Parthenon, we sat at a long wood table, enjoying a delightful brunch buffet. The conversation rambled at high speed like a happily drunk speedboat at sea. We had no agenda and no one tried to create one. No one took notes except for my occasional list making in my notebook.

Meetings at Automattic were always qualified disasters. They happened so rarely, certainly in-person ones, and had so little urgency there was little pressure to get better at running them. Most of the world has deadlines. If you don't have deadlines, the need to be good at efficient decision making fades away. Without schedules and budgets, there were rarely decisions with permanent consequences, and Mullenweg made most high-stakes decisions. As a result, meetings followed the same rambling style as P2 conversations did, with few rules. On a P2, anyone can raise any comment at any time, and everyone else is free to ignore it or respond to it. There were rarely hard end points and little interest in finding them. One school of meetings is to simply list an agenda of questions so the meeting has a spine to hold it together, but the meeting that morning didn't have one of those either.

As we relaxed in the warm Mediterranean sun, we jumped between discussions of company strategy, to coding methods, to feature ideas, to bugs we'd seen, to gossip about other teams, and back again. It was fun and inspiring. At the most primal level, this was good-natured smart people who care about the same things talking with each other—the kind of chemistry that executives spend careers trying, and mostly failing, to create. And beneath it all was the sensation of Athens. Who has team meetings in Athens? Who gets on a plane to meet with coworkers in ATHENS? It was continual background energy for the whole meet-up, the visceral sense we were all together in a good place, with good food and quality of work life in every way provided for us. It never entirely made sense to me why we were there, but the effect of it was clear: we were all energized, inspired, and ready to earn our trip to an amazing place.

My immediate challenge was doing my job as lead inside the chaos. The dialogue was great, but as the person accountable for making sure Team Social shipped good work, the increasing number of open threads made me uncomfortable. As I explained in previous chapters, ideas were not our problem. A countdown clock was ticking in my brain for when to force major decisions to closure. What was the vision for our team? What big goals would we sign up for? I wanted to decide this in Athens, as a team with Matt in person. I wanted us to make big bets and show the company we could have visions of cathedrals and build them with bazaar methods. What I didn't want was to spend days riffing on yet more ideas, only to return home was as much ambiguity as when we'd arrived. The bottleneck is never code or creativity; it's lack of clarity.

One big decision we needed to make was about the future of comments, the primary feature for readers of a blog to respond to what the blogger had published. With our goal of helping users be more active, comments were critical. Nearly 300,000 comments were published every day on WordPress.com, and we wanted to improve the design so more visitors would write them. The challenge was that we had had two different technologies:

- WordPress.com's built-in commenting system
- IntenseDebate, a commenting plug-in acquired by Automattic in 2009 that worked on WordPress and on competing blog software

IntenseDebate was popular, but it was built in an entirely different way than WordPress.com was. They shared no code, so any improvements we made to one had to be done a second time on the other. This was a problem. For strategic investments, you don't want to have to continually do the same work twice. If we wanted commenting to be central to our strategy, we had three options:

A. Invest in both ID and WordPress.com comments.
B. Invest only in Intense Debate.
C. Invest only in WordPress.com comments.

A and B made little sense. Investing only in IntenseDebate, a product that could never directly improve WordPress.com, was foolish. Option C was the only viable one. I knew Beau and Adams probably agreed, but Matt was harder to read. We'd discussed it at length over Skype and understood the options, but he was more optimistic than I was. IntenseDebate was the one offering that worked on competing systems and therefore protected our flank. That's why Automattic had acquired it. The acquisition made sense, but you never invest more in your flank than your front line. If you did, you'd always be defensive, not offensive.

Later at brunch, I made my case. I pitched hard for option C: the goal should be one code base and one design that we reused in many places. Although it would take time for WordPress.com comments to catch up to the features in IntenseDebate, the length of time was irrelevant. Once it was unified, every improvement made would be reused everywhere. There wasn't much discussion: we all quickly agreed on the plan I'd offered. We'd do tactical improvements to IntenseDebate in the short term and then focus on WordPress.com. We left the question of the future of IntenseDebate open since we didn't need to decide immediately.

Later that afternoon while walking through the agora where Socrates had walked, we dubbed this mission to unify comments Highlander, a reference to the classic sci-fi film where knights fight each other until only one survives. I'm certain my team had no idea it was an old Microsoft joke. Any project designed to replace two others was always called Highlander, and given how many competing projects there often were, many projects shared that name. Jokes aside, the decisions focused us. The rambling discussions and wide-ranging ideas came up less often now that our energy was aimed on a big problem—a challenge large enough it might take months or even years to finish. We were quite pleased, but had no idea how much trouble we'd just created for ourselves.

CHAPTER 13

DOUBLE DOWN

Even if I'd had a complaint about my employer, it'd have been hard to remember what it was while walking up the steps to the Parthenon. Listed as one of the greatest works of architecture in the world, the Parthenon resides on the glorious Acropolis, a plateau rising five hundred feet above Athens. At night the hillside and the buildings are lit up, and from our hotel windows, we could see it hovering above the city, like a Magritte painting of a mountain fortress floating in the sky. In reading the guidebooks, I learned that when the Parthenon was built, it was covered in bright colors, and the aged marble we associate with ancient things is an artifact of age, not of design. Curiously, the restoration during our visit did not include any plans to restore the bright greens and yellows of its original style. Everyone expects ruins to look like ruins, so the restoration will restore our image of the past, proving again that objective history is elusive, if possible at all.

The Parthenon is of course undeniably beautiful, but more than its aesthetics, I was impressed by the achievement of its construction. As a leader of an engineering team, I found it hard not to consider the many challenges of carefully moving 100,000 tons of fragile marble from a quarry ten miles away up to the high plateau, two thousand years ago, centuries before power tools, electric lights, or cold beer.[1] It's no surprise that slave labor was part of the answer, as it must have been grueling work.

It's never a surprise in great projects to find grueling work somewhere along the way—work that never upholds the same aesthetic as the final results. Tales of the hard parts often fail to make it into the brochures or the corporate tours. Steve Jobs's obsession with making the interiors of Apple's products look beautiful, even though no one would see them, always struck me as curious but strange. Most of the ancient and Renaissance masters he admired didn't feel the same way. It sometimes takes ugly effort to make beautiful things. People who love great things but are ignorant of how they're made are mystified by how dirty they have to get their own hands to make anything at all: they think the mess means they're doing something wrong, when mostly it just means they're finally doing real work. This isn't to say you should deliberately create mess and chaos (that'd be silly), but to fear it as a sure sign of error shows ignorance and nothing more.

Our decision to go for Highlander (the plan for a single commenting system) forced tough choices, most of which we couldn't yet see. When Automattic acquired IntenseDebate in 2008 its founders, Isaac Keyet and Jon Fox, joined the company. By 2010 they had moved on to other projects, and Beau picked it up. It was common for people to move between projects at Automattic, the philosophy being that movement was the only way to spread knowledge and simultaneously keep people challenged to keep learning. IntenseDebate earned a reputation with many Automatticians for being fragile to work with, even just when installing it on their own blogs. The code bases engineers work with suffer from reputations just like people do, and they're hard to shake. As a result, few at Automattic were interested in working on IntenseDebate.

Beau, like the good trooper he was, took it on without much complaint. According to Beau, the way it was architected made common bugs hard to fix. He'd become adept at patching those issues, but they took time and it was frustrating, uninteresting work. The project wasn't built in the same way as the rest of WordPress.com. Often acquisitions create a paradox: they're hard to fit into a company for the same reason they're attractive to acquire. The thing you want to buy reflects a different way of thinking, which has value, but that difference is at odds with the culture you already have. Like an organ transplant, natural antibodies will fight against having the new organ fit in. And the more you do to force it in, the less of what you wanted to acquire in the first place remains. The vast majority of acquisitions fail for this reason. Few executives recognize the paradox, or think themselves immune to it.

Highlander would require months of effort, assuming my whole team worked on it full time, which was impossible. Just to maintain features already live took 20 to 40 percent of our time for bug fixes, performance issues, and other problems that naturally arise with large-scale services (we didn't know precisely how much time we spent on maintenance, since no one tracked their hours).

This left us two choices for how to manage IntenseDebate:

A. *Be responsive.* Wait for issues to arise and respond as needed. These problems were urgent, complex, and disruptive when they happened, but they might not happen often if we prayed to the right gods.
B. *Be proactive.* Invest two weeks now in improving IntenseDebate's weak spots to reduce the odds of new problems.

This decision point is universal. Do you fix that tire with the slow leak? Do you get that achy elbow looked at now, or hope it goes away? I've heard experts on decisions like these proclaim perfect formulas for these daily situations, but I can tell you there isn't one—unless of course you have a time machine. And if you have a time machine, you don't need to worry about any of your decisions: if you don't like an outcome, you just go back and do it over. Without the time machine, all choices have the possibility of being wrong. Your model of the universe can be a perfect model of the past, but the past is not a reliable predictor of the future because there is no such thing. Some models are more reliable than others, but black swans can shatter any of them. And sometimes your model can be deeply flawed, yet by sheer luck it works out all right. The best you can do is evaluate the odds, weigh alternatives, boldly move forward, and repeat. Since Highlander wasn't urgent, there was little cost for delaying in favor of shoring up IntenseDebate. We went with option B.

Part of the reason that perfect decision formulas can't exist is that you never know if you're buying too much or too little insurance. Did you see the right doctor for your elbow? Did you ask the right questions? You can make the correct decision in the wrong way. One risk with our plan B was that two weeks wasn't enough. We might need to spend months to improve even one weak spot. Fear of this uncertainty motivates people to spin their wheels for days considering all the possible outcomes, calculating them in a spreadsheet using utility cost analysis or some other fancy method that even the guy who invented it doesn't use. But all that analysis just keeps you on the sidelines. Often you're better off flipping a coin and moving in any clear direction. Once you start moving, you get new data regardless of where you're trying to go. And the new data makes the next decision and the next better than staying on the sidelines desperately trying to predict the future without that time machine.

What I needed but didn't have was a way to evaluate IntenseDebate's code. Like many other young companies, Automattic had no formal quality assurance. Barry and the systems team did an excellent job keeping WordPress.com up and the servers running, but at the feature level, the level of code running on those servers, teams were on their own. Years ago I'd worked on real-time systems projects like IntenseDebate, but we had diagnostic tools to isolate problems and test changes. Automattic had no such tools, and few people had experience in making or using them.

Generally I liked this about Automattic. The absence of dedicated quality assurance people made every employee accountable for quality, which is rare if there are many QA people around. Start-up cultures and small teams are fantastic at making everyone help since you can't hide behind job titles: there's too much work to be done. Like remodeling an entire house with a friend, pretense drops. Everyone is expected to grab a paintbrush or haul some trash. In the old days, Microsoft used to deliberately understaff teams to help keep pretense and BS low. Too much understaffing causes misery, but if you cut it right and delegate ownership liberally, morale and productivity stay high. Passionate people love to feel like empowered underdogs.

I realized the two weeks might return nothing but a scouting report, but it would show me two things at once, which I liked. The first would be a good look at the code itself. It would push Beau, with fresh eyes from Peatling and Adams, to evaluate things differently. He wouldn't be working alone, and that changed everything. The second thing we'd learn was how Team Social worked on an unpopular, fuzzy, possibly wicked problem. Learning about this second perspective was critical to my role. It helped me answer these questions:

- What was our team like under pressure?
- Who could I count on?
- Who got frustrated first?
- Which programmer would set the pace?

We were too young as a team for me to know. And since we'd all agreed we'd reevaluate the plan after the first two-week cycle, I had little to lose. I was comfortable flipping the switch on a possible runaway train if I knew I had another switch a mile up the track to shut things down.

The prevailing attitude at Automattic was that any big project is simply a series of smaller ones, and I liked this. It avoids the stupid things that happen on projects by never allowing you to fall in love with your grand plans. As the joke goes, if you don't have a plan, then you never worry if your plan is wrong. And as the pithy saying goes, the map is not the territory. If you make an elaborate map, you forget the world may change for the worse while you're staring at your beautiful little map. People drive off cliffs and into lakes because their GPS device told them there was a road, but there wasn't. Without the GPS, that can't happen.

In project terms, if you make only small maps, of, say, the next two weeks, you never run the risk of your map being very wrong, and you learn more from the present since it has your full attention. Many trendy management techniques make much of this discovery, but it's old news. Entrepreneurs, squad leaders in any military organization in history, and artists of all kinds figured this out long ago. But even advocates of small plans get it wrong too. You should never be religious about methods of any kind. The only sane way to work is to let the project define the plan. Only a fool chooses tools before studying the job to be done.

But the downside to working in small increments, the way of the web and Automattic, is that stupid things can happen because of the absence of forethought. By forethought, I mean thinking through, for even a handful of hours, how all the parts must fit together, or considering which parts are hardest and doing those first to ensure the project is viable at all. There is little worse than working on something in small increments for months, only to discover, near the end, that the only solution for the last increment requires redoing everything you've done so far. Or, as was the case with many Microsoft products, and now WordPress too, many little features, each designed on its own, compete for attention at the expense of the customer's experience.

Like the decision about Highlander and IntenseDebate, there is no perfect answer. After years of leading projects, the best thing I've learned is that I have to periodically shift between thinking small (bazaar) and thinking long term (cathedral). Asking my team, "If we do these three features in a row, how do they build together into something better than the sum of the parts?" I don't want them fixated on thinking that far ahead, but I do want them to raise their heads and look to the horizon periodically, because that glance improves how they'll evaluate whatever they're building today.

Before we'd even begun on Highlander, our ambitions got the better of us. Another grand project that had been floated by Mullenweg was something he called ".org connect." He'd talked about it enough that other Automatticians referred to it on P2s and in IRC. I'd overhear in conversations, "When we have .org connect, we'll be able to do this," or, "We shouldn't build that until we have .org connect," as if it had solid form in this universe. It did not. Not a single programmer had lifted a finger to even start thinking about how to build it. This kind of vaporware speculation drove me crazy. Most of Automattic was too young to realize vaporware can go on for years with people endlessly believing in something no one is working on, preventing plenty of good plans from starting because of an unchallenged mythology.

However, the idea itself was brilliant, which is why its popularity exceeded its reality. In short, Mullenweg wanted a bridge between any WordPress blog and the special features that currently worked only if a blog was hosted on WordPress.com (e.g., the subscription notifications e-mails my team built could work only for blogs that lived on WordPress.com). There were 60 million WordPress blogs in the world, but half were hosted on services like DreamHost, Media Temple, and GoDaddy. With the bridge, the enhanced features of WordPress.com would be available to all WordPress blogs in the world. This would be a win for those bloggers, as they'd have more powerful software for free. It'd be a win for WordPress, as the platform would be stronger. And it would be a win for WordPress.com, as it would introduce many WordPress users to WordPress.com for the first time. If Highlander was bringing two things into one, this bridge would kill three birds with a single stone. This set my little team lead heart aflutter.

I pushed hard for Team Social to take on the project. We had Adams and Lebens, two programmers with the right skills, and many of the existing WordPress.com features that would go best across that bridge my team was responsible for (Publicize, Subscriptions, and Post by Email). While there was logic to this, my ambition was foolish. Highlander was more than enough for us to do for months, if not years. On the team we'd often use the term *double down*, from the card game blackjack, when we had a tricky decision to make. We all believed making the bet bigger solved many problems since it forced you to fight through a challenge rather than sneak around it—and making a commitment to build .org connect was the biggest bet any team at the company could make.

There was no debate. We all agreed that Team Social should take it on. But there were no practical considerations. When would we start? No idea. How would it work? No idea. But those concerns never came up, as they rarely do when young men get lost in their own ideas. To start big projects, you must have the capacity for delusion. All the rational people, despite their brilliance, are too reasonable to start crazy things. And working against us in this sense was that we'd spent the day walking in the footsteps of Socrates, Plato, and Aristotle, spurring us all to believe in our grandest dreams.

That night we went out to a great evening of Dionysian delights. Stefanos Kofopoulos, a local friend of Matt, was our host, and he led us out into a glorious trail of pubs, bars, and eateries. Nikolay Bachiyski, the lead for the NUX team, had flown in from Bulgaria earlier in the day and joined in. As we ate, debated, and brainstormed our way into the night, the recurring challenge was to find a name for the "org project." Round and round the ideas went, from The Connector, to WordBridge, to dozens of variants and wordplays, none striking a chord. Beau eventually offered Jetpack, which we liked, but not enough to stop trying alternatives. As the night wore on, though, the name sounded better and better, and soon it stuck. Late that night when we finally went to bed, we all slept well having chosen, and named, the two important projects that would define ourselves and our team.

CHAPTER 14

THERE CAN BE ONLY ONE

One of our first running jokes as a team was about ouzo. No one remembers how or why, but one night out with Stefanos, Nikolay, and Matt, we wanted to do a round of drinks to celebrate and asked our waitress about Athens's local alcohols. Ouzo was mentioned, and I said I hated it. Immediately everyone clambered for us to do a round of ouzo shots, which we did, several times, yelling, "Ouzo!" It was ironic and stupid, but we all laughed. I'm sure I ordered rounds myself, as the joke got better as the trip went on. But later, even we got sick of not only drinking ouzo but talking about it. We made a rule: any mention of ouzo meant the person who said it had to stop whatever he was doing and have a shot. By Team Social law, I now owe six shots of the stuff for this paragraph alone.

Laughter paves the way for many things. It's one way to build intimacy between people, something every healthy team needs. Humor has always been a primary part of how I lead. If I can get someone to laugh, they're at ease. If they see me laugh at things, they're at ease. It creates emotional space, a kind of trust, to use in a relationship. Sharing laughter also creates a bank account of positive energy you can withdraw from, or borrow against, when dealing with tough issues at work. It's a relationship cushion. The good fortune for me was that Beau, Adams, Peatling, and I liked making each other laugh. Often that went to offensive lengths, but laugh we did anyway. Automattic at large was a place with many running jokes, and sharp, clever sarcasm was found in most P2 and IRC conversations. Team Social's flavor was more twisted and juvenile, but if that was your thing, we were by far the most fun team to be around.

Laughter leads to running jokes, and running jokes lead to a shared history, and a shared history is culture. What is a friend, a brother or sister, or a partner but someone you share important stories with? Families, tribes, and teams all function in similar ways, building bonds through rites of passages and shared experiences. In extreme situations, people sacrifice their lives for their culture. While cultures form organically, someone has to be the instigator and get things in motion, reinforcing the good and reducing the bad. In many ways, this was me, always looking for little ways to improve the odds. But it was always clear to me that the master facilitator of culture was Mullenweg.

If ever you wonder about why a family or a company is the way it is, always look up first. The culture in any organization is shaped every day by the behavior of the most powerful person in the room. If at your job, people yell at each other often, the reason it happens is that the most powerful person in the room lets it happen. He or she hired the person who's yelling—and failed to interrupt that person or pull him or her aside for feedback about that behavior. If the powerful person did choose to act, it would stop, even if the choice had to be firing the offender.

In every meeting in every organization around the world where bad behavior is happening, there is someone with the most power in the room who can do something about it. What that person does shapes the culture. If the most powerful person is silent, this signals passive acceptance of whatever is going on. And if that person speaks up to say, "Good idea," or, "Thanks for asking a clarifying question," everyone notices and will be more likely to do those things. It's deep in human nature to look to the top to define our own behavior, even at a company as autonomous as Automattic.

Whether on a P2, an IRC chat, or a Skype conversation, someone involved has the best reputation and most influence and chooses to use it or not. Those choices accumulate into what outsiders call culture.

While I take some credit for instigating Team Social's shenanigans and turning a blind but laughing eye to ones started by my teammates, Mullenweg enabled it all. Not once in Athens did he correct my behavior, question how we were spending our time, or use his authority to contradict our decisions. In Athens he embodied the ideal leadership role Toni Schneider imagined, separating the people making the product from the people supporting the makers, almost to a fault. I was empowered by Mullenweg. If my team failed, I was comfortable taking complete responsibility because I had been granted room to make the team my own. While I'd seen with other projects in the company that Mullenweg could have a heavy hand when he wanted one, I hadn't experienced it myself, at least not yet. Athens was a fantastic time for Team Social. Our identity solidified. And I assumed it was a fulfillment of Matt's vision for what a meet-up was supposed to be or, perhaps even better, his providing us space to define it for ourselves.

It's quite a thing to be in meetings in person with Matt. There's a calm to him that surprises most people given how much power and influence he has. He often speaks softly and with a smile. He laughs easily and likes to laugh. At times he can be quiet, and he is hard to read when he is, but there's a general charm and good-natured warmth about him. He doesn't fit the CEO/founder profile of wanting to be the center of attention at all times. Instead he's an excellent dinner host at outings, full of southern hospitality, making sure everyone is taken care of with food or drink or conversation. I've learned quite a few things from him in how to carry myself in semisocial situations. I'd never had a boss before who so naturally took care of the people around him. He has a generosity of spirit that is undeniably sincere, and it comes across in the large, when he's on stage as the leader of the WordPress mission, but also in the small, when you're with him and a handful of others, sharing a few beers. All the success he'd had hadn't changed him from what I imagine he was like as a younger man.

In meetings in person, he loves to let things flow and develop organically. I don't know if this trait influenced the WordPress culture or if the way WordPress developed influenced him. Or both. I imagine his years studying jazz saxophone played a role as well, as he has an unusual patience for letting things wander. At the same time, there's a hint of shyness to him—a trace of the introversion that many creatives and programmers who have become famous never lose. I've often thought that hint explains why he's happy working at company where most of his interaction with people is filtered by technology. There's a degree of control that the filter of technology gives you—a control that introverts often prefer. The centricity of those filters in most of the important relationships in his life enables freedoms most people would never imagine.

Since he can manage his company from anywhere, he is often in flight around the world. More than two hundred days a year, he is somewhere other than San Francisco, the place he technically calls home. It was always fun when chatting with him on Skype and guessing where in the world he was or what time it might be there. This freedom has either fueled, or been fueled by, the curiosity of his renaissance mind. From survival courses to exotic travel, he has an epicurean desire to experience and understand all the great things of being alive. Part of his vision, a vision some employees follow, is to take full advantage of being able to work from anywhere to truly work anywhere. Travel for teams to meet up in places like Athens was directly in line with that vision.

Matt didn't worry much about time or structure, which made sticking to an agenda in a meeting with him unlikely. It's a common habit of CEOs: they spend so much of their day with people vying for their attention that there's little need to for them to worry about schedules. Their schedule gets defined largely by everyone else's demands. But unlike most other CEOs I've known, he possesses uncommon patience. He rarely checked his phones or gadgets. When he was in the room, he was fully present and generous with his attention. He listened. More so, he was an amazing manager of his personal time and attention.[1] The number of e-mails, P2s, Skype conversations, blogs, and industry events he followed and participated in was mind boggling. And he was an avid reader too. All this told me he had a disciplined and flexible mind and great control over how, when, and where he applied it. The fact that he exerted little effort to control and shape Team Social's meet-up was his choice. I didn't know how he handled other teams, but it was clear he deliberately let us define things ourselves.

If you had joined us when Stefanos took us out for a fun night on the town, hosting us in his country in the best possibly way, you'd have had trouble guessing Mullenweg was my boss, much less the company founder. We looked like a bunch of college friends a few years past graduation, out on vacation. The challenge with Mullenweg was how different his persona came across online. On Skype or IRC, all of the secondary feedback people give each other were gone. You know only the words they type. He'd earned a reputation for being terse, occasionally cryptic, and, to some, quite intimidating online. In the WordPress world, he often referred to himself as a benevolent dictator, which works great if you have similar opinions but can be painful when you don't. What confused newer employees was trying to correlate these two Matts—the one they'd met at a WordCamp, all charm and quiet warmth, with the one they'd get feedback from on P2s, which was terse and cold. As the company grew and demands on Matt's time increased, his ability to participate in decisions fell, contributing to the terseness others experienced. The creation of teams was intended to foster more local autonomy and less dependence on Matt, but at the time of the Athens meet-up, teams were only weeks old.

When Mullenweg left Athens, we immediately began work on Highlander. Of the many features we knew it would have to include, we narrowed them down to find the simplest, easiest, highest-value project we could release first (what's often called MVP or minimum viable product). Putting our list of feature ideas aside for the moment, we applied the same design thinking we'd done for posting.

If the blogger's experience posting worked like this:

Draft Post → Edit → Publish → See how the world responds

then the visitor's experience commenting was like this:

Read Post → Decide to comment → Type in Comment →

Hit Submit → See response

The largest burden of convincing a visitor to decide to comment was on the blogger. Bloggers who wrote a better post were more likely to get visitors to write comments in response. But anything we could do to help the process was worth doing.

The first step for every would-be commenter was to put in contact information, something WordPress required. Our MVP was therefore to simplify the process by letting commenters use Facebook or Twitter accounts to skip those steps. We'd do Facebook first since that service had many more users than Twitter did. The design question was how to best arrange the order and position of everything.

Designing is best done first on paper. It's cheap and fast, making it easy to try many ideas well before anyone's ego is invested. While Adams and Beau worked on the architecture we'd need no matter what the design was, Peatling and I worked on layouts. We quickly tried one with the comment area on top, another with it on the bottom, a third with it on the side, and so on. These differences seem small, but when you have millions of people using a design every day, a 1 or 2 percent difference in how many people comment is significant. We thought carefully about how users would step through the process with the different designs and picked the strongest one, agreeing we could easily experiment more later, live on WordPress.com. I added details to the design, while Peatling started coding. At the same time, Adams and Beau divided up the two ends of connecting WordPress.com to Facebook, planning to meet in the middle. We were off and running down in the lobby of the Electra Hotel (which you may recall was the opening scene of this book).

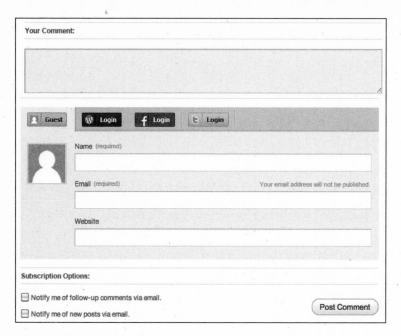

On the surface, this design seems easy. It's a few buttons, and anyone can build a button. The challenge was all the things that happen behind the scenes to let users make it work simply when a visitor clicked that button. We had to securely pass data across many different systems, including the blog itself, Facebook, and WordPress.com's servers. As we discussed how all the pieces would have to fit together to create a good user experience, dozens of notes, issues, and questions accumulated, We shaped them into work items and made a list on our P2.

We worked nonstop for three days, breaking mostly for biology. We'd head to the balcony bar at night to unwind, staying until they kicked us out at 2:00 a.m. I'm confident we spent more on

Mythos and chips each night than most of their other customers that day combined.

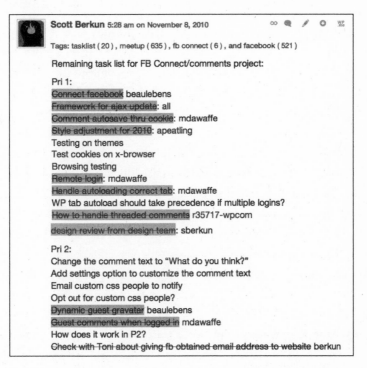

In the lobby, our working style was indistinguishable from how we worked when miles apart. We all had IRC windows open in the background, Skype on the side. We'd ask questions and pass links to each other in IRC to look at bugs or designs. Sometimes someone would start a conversation out loud, but we were mostly mode indifferent, switching between digital and nondigital easily. Occasionally someone slid his laptop screen over to someone to show something, which garnered faster feedback than sending a Skype and waiting for him to get to it. But mostly you could have teleported us to different corners of the planet, and provided there was wi-fi, we'd continuing working without a hitch. Beau played his music, and we all sang along. When someone finished a task, he'd mark it off on the P2 and grab another or ask me what to do or who to help. The big bet of Highlander raised our morale: for the first time, it wasn't just a feature we were building but part of a large, strategic goal for the company.

But in spite of our esprit de corps, one day the annoyances of the lobby became too much. It was louder than before, and the ugly couches were somehow even less comfortable. I hunted for alternative locales, but there were no coworking spaces to rent nearby, limiting us to the hotel. I got permission to use the seemingly quiet hallway near the conference rooms on the second floor, securing tables and power strips. But an hour later, we were distracted by the constant noise from the lobby: a film crew of some kind, with what appeared to be a few fashion models, set up in the lobby. We'd learn they were filming something for *Top Chef Athens;* at least that was the rumor among the staff. As if that wasn't enough, soon a woman, whom we were never sure was staff or a guest, paced past our tables with the loudest cell phone ring we'd ever heard, and as she finally made her way down the hall, we'd hear the ring again and again, just loud enough to be impossible to ignore, making us laugh each time we heard it. It was frustrating at the time to realize we'd traveled from around the world to be here, when we might have been more productive if we were all at home.

We hit rock bottom that afternoon when Adams's laptop started to fail, dropping its connection to the hotel wi-fi, forcing him to restart his machine every fifteen minutes—just enough time for him to figure out where he was before the last restart. Watching his computer convert his life into a scene from the film *Groundhog Day* was depressing to witness, much less experience. Our varied miseries combined made me realize I'd underplanned the meet-up. With no guide to follow, I had made rookie mistakes. For future meet-ups I'd ensure at least one reliable, quiet, well-powered room, with good wi-fi, that we could use whenever we wanted. Our meet-up time together was too precious to allow trivial annoyances like these to get in the way. I also made a note to nag Adams to buy a new laptop when he got home.

Beyond all of the problems of our environment, we'd hit a more fundamental challenge. The fun part of the project was over, and the ego boost from working on something new and important had faded. We'd fallen into the classic project trap, the trap that makes the ends harder than the beginnings.

Projects accumulate a pile of annoying tasks people postpone, but in order to ship the product, that pile must be emptied. Things that are less fun to do are usually harder to do, which means the pile isn't ordinary work but a pile of unloved, unwanted, complex work:

1. We do things we like first.
2. We do things we don't like last.
3. The things we don't like tend to be harder.
4. Late changes have cascading effects.

This means that at the end of any project, you're left with a pile of things no one wants to do and are the hardest to do (or, worse, no one is quite sure how to do them). It should never be a surprise that progress seems to slow as the finish line approaches, even if everyone is working just as hard as they were before. With forty-eight hours left in our meet-up, we admitted we were out of time to launch the first part of Highlander from Athens. We went through our lists as a team, cleaning up our notes on our P2. I wanted this to be tidy since we didn't know how long it would be until we returned to finish.

I had no idea how right I was.

CHAPTER 15

THE FUTURE OF WORK, PART 2

The title of this book is a reference to a running joke that appeared on Team Social's P2. No one is sure how it started, but the pants reference appeared on our P2's changeable prompt. Few noticed it, since by default it said something civilized like, "What's on your mind?" or, "How can Team Social help you?" and when it changed, they didn't notice. But for many months it said: "Do you know where your pants are?"

Pants, or lack thereof, came up often on conversations on our P2, as this conversation from February 2011 captures:

Mdawaffe (Adams): Apparently Nikolay doesn't know yet of our team's predilection for working without pants.
Beau: I thought it was a requirement? P.S. time for a new laptop
Nikolay: With pants everything is boring

Mdawaffe: Disproof by contradiction: Dinosaurs with pants are not boring

Nikolay: Math rhetoric FTW! I declare defeat.

Working remotely is the first thing many people learn about Automattic. They assume it's a sham. It violates the bright yellow line that we pretend exists between work and home, a line shattered by laptops and mobile e-mail years ago. As I pointed out earlier in the book, remote work, and many other perks Automattic used, will work or fail because of company culture, not because of the perk itself. Since by now you know how my team functioned, in this chapter I'll explore the general challenges with working distributedly and without e-mail.

I'm certain of the following:

- Self-motivated people thrive when granted independence.
- Managers who want better performance must provide what their staff needs.

Remote work is a kind of trust, and trust works two ways. Recently Yahoo CEO Marissa Mayer banned remote work from her company, claiming it made people less productive.[1] She might have been right: in her company, people may have abused the trust that remote work grants employees. Some employees abuse free office supplies from the copy room. Others lie about taking sick days. Every benefit granted can be used to perform better work, or it can be abused. The benefit itself rarely has much to do with it. If someone who works for you wants to work remotely or use a new e-mail tool or brainstorming method, little is lost in letting him or her try it out. If his or her performance stays the same or improves, you win. If it goes poorly, you still win, as you've demonstrated your willingness to experiment, encouraging everyone who works for you to continue looking for ways to improve their performance. They become allies in making you look good, because you're simply willing to try. If someone suggests thirty-minute instead of sixty-minute meetings, what is there to lose? If the experiment fails, you end it and try another.

But despite what they say, most people fear new ideas. They instinctively defend the old, no matter how frustrated they are with it. A common refrain I've heard is, "If I let one person do [insert possible good thing here], everyone will want to do it," as if somehow the pillars of an organization will crumble if anything ever changes. The oldest, largest companies today all began much like Automattic, with ambitious youth, big ideas, and high thresholds for change. It's the ambition and flexibility that enabled them to do well enough to grow old in the first place. If you want longevity, you can't just bet on tradition; you have to continually invest in the future.

As research for this book, I read many studies on trends in remote work. Many of them point to a steady stream of adoption. The *Economist* reported a survey of eleven thousand workers around the world, with nearly 20 percent working remotely often and 7 percent full time.[2] I found dozens of companies structured like Automattic, designed for distributed work.[3] Of course you won't find auto mechanics, restaurants, or zoologists on this list because their work demands their being in the same physical place all of the time. But for any office where people spend most of their time in e-mail and on web browsers, the door is open to try something new. Tom Preston Warner, chief technology officer of GitHub, a popular collaboration tool, believes that any organization that works primarily in the digital world can work remotely.[4] Like Automattic, GitHub has always been a fully distributed company, naturally reaching many of the same conclusions as Automattic about autonomy, empowerment, and trust.

Outsiders assume remote work means working from home, but that's an important inaccuracy. The true directive is that employees can locate themselves wherever they want. You could work from your back deck. Or you could rent an office in a coworking space or travel around South America in a used Jeep with good wi-fi. In all cases it is *up to you as an employee to figure out how to be productive.* This is true everywhere, of course, but with less structure from management, there are fewer places to hide bad habits. For people with poor discipline, this freedom can be a problem, just as any other kind of freedom can be.

Many new employees at Automattic spend months adjusting to the change. They can't as easily base their schedule on their coworkers. They won't have a boss reminding them hourly to get certain tasks done. And most powerful of all, the social structures of coffee breaks, lunch chats, and happy hours are gone, forcing employees to build more of their own social life if they need one. I have adjusted to these issues fine (writers are good at solitary work), but there was one I never overcame: lingering doubts about where I stood in the company. In a normal workplace, you sense how well you fit in by how often people seek you out, and you can compare that to the conversations you observe others having without you. But online, there is no way to calibrate. You never see the Skype chats you're not in. Remote work demands social proactivity. Some talented people find these freedoms overwhelming, preferring the structure of space and time that traditional offices provide.

Curious about how Automatticians felt about these issues, I did a poll on the Updates P2 asking where people worked (the company provided a subsidy for any employee who wanted to rent office space). From the ninety people who responded the results were clear:

	OVERALL
In my home / home office	60.4%
At coffee shops	17.82%
At an actual office	8.91%
In hotels / airplanes	6.93%
At a co-working space	3.96%
Other:	1.98%

About a third of the company had children, and working remotely helped them manage the logistical challenges of raising children. Much like college students, they could be free to arrange their work schedules to fit their lives rather than constantly struggling with the pull of one against another.

In October 2012, after I left Automattic, I polled my blog readers asking how many would work remotely if they could.[5] Of the 524 who responded, 338 already worked from home. This was not a surprise, since many of my blog readers work in technology where remote work is common. Of the 341 who currently worked in a traditional office, 64 percent said they'd like to give working from home a try. A vocal minority had tried it but found that the lack of division between home and work made them less productive. No work environment works for everyone: strict boundaries help some people manage their lives.

LIFE WITHOUT E-MAIL

When I say that Automattic doesn't use e-mail, people lift an eyebrow as if I'd said the company doesn't believe in oxygen or bans the use of the letter E. Every employee has an e-mail account; they're just rarely used. Despite constant complaints about endless piles of e-mail in the business world, there is a fatalism about alternatives. It's surprising to find this defeatist, status-quo attitude among progressives and early adopters given how old e-mail is: it's older than the web itself by more than a decade. All tools are good for some tasks and bad for others. If a technology annoys you, it probably has more to do with how the people around you use it than the technology itself.

E-mail madness, or e-mailopathy, is the name I have for the psychological disorder where people are so overwhelmed by the waves of e-mail they receive that they protect their psyche by never reading any of it. Instead they skim e-mails quickly and write and send replies even quicker, like a paranoid, drunk blindfolded man pulling the trigger of a fully loaded AK-47. What they don't realize is if they send waves of bad e-mail out, they're guaranteed to get waves of bad e-mail back, especially if the person on the other end has the same disorder they do. If Pascal, who once wrote, "If I had more time I'd write a shorter letter," had to contend with this, he'd have said, "If I read incoming e-mails carefully, the e-mails I send will generate fewer replies." Alas, for all our technological progress, we still have yet to invent anything that increases reading comprehension. Remember that culture changes the value of tools: for example, if you have a team of people who hate each other, they will make each other miserable no matter how many billions of dollars of communication technology they use. Alternatively if you have people who trust each other and have similar goals, they'll be effective with smoke signals and carrier pigeons. Wars have been won by tightly knit armies using candles and Morse code.

Technology does have an impact on behavior, but culture comes first. An easily overlooked factor is that most Automatticians have tangible jobs: writing code, designing screens, answering tickets. They're not in the stressful limbo of abstraction that middle managers and consultants live in. Instead there's little posturing or showing off. People who know how to build things don't worry about turf. They know they can always make more. It's often people whose jobs are abstractions that see a company as a zero-sum game where they have to fight and defend what's theirs to stay alive or get promoted. Most discussions at Automattic were about how to build, design, or fix some specific tangible thing. That pragmatism changes the nature of how people communicate. There were few turf battles, approval seekings, or the grandstanding that dominate many miserable e-mail threads.

E-mail has rarely discussed disadvantages:

- *E-mail empowers the sender.* They can put in your inbox whatever they like and as many times as they like (many receivers use filters and rules as countermeasures).
- *E-mail is a closed channel.* There's no way to see an e-mail if you are not on the "to" list, forcing work groups to err on the side of

including everyone. Only a fraction of e-mail has direct relevance to any particular person.

- *E-mail decays over time.* If someone writes a great e-mail, an employee has to do something to preserve it. Otherwise it sits in an inbox, hidden from new employees. Over time, that organizational knowledge fades away.

P2s by design invert these assumptions:

- The reader, not the sender, chooses what to read.
- The reader chooses how often and in what form he or she wants to read.
- Since P2s are a form of blog, they're easy to skim, easy to reference with a URL, available to all forever, searchable, and easily pushed into different reading tools.

One secret at Automattic is that e-mail is technically part of how P2s work: it is used for notifications. In any post on a P2, you can add a command to notify someone you want them to read it. For example, I might write in a post, "hey @peatling can you give me your opinion?" The P2 would automatically look up in a database who @peatling is and send him a notification in e-mail. The conversation stays on the P2, but e-mail helps bring it to the attention of whomever the author desired.

```
[automattcher] Mike Adams (mdawaffe) on The Bureau of Social...
Automattcher
  Sent: April 24, 2011 8:43 PM
    To: info@scottberkun.com

http://socialp2.wordpress.com/2013/04/25/hi-sberkun-can-you-please-send-me-your/
Match: /@\bsberkun\b/i

Mike Adams (mdawaffe):
Hi, @sberkun. Can you please send me your TPS report?  It's long overdue.
```

I loved P2s. They put me in control of how I consumed everything on my team and across the company. But I did notice its downsides. In July 2011, having observed symptoms of P2 abuse,

I wrote a long post called "The Limits of P2." It lauded the tool but called out bad habits we'd fallen into because we liked it so much. What's interesting is if you changed the title to "The Limits of E-mail" it works just as well:

1. *Some conversations need to be real time.* Brainstorming and teaching require high interactivity, but blogs are designed for latency. If you are exploring an idea, or debugging something, and want the best possible communication, go real time (IRC/Skype).

2. *Voice has more data.* We are a text-centric culture here, but voices have more data. We get tons of information (humor, attitude, nuance) you can't get from text. When in doubt, go voice. A 20 post P2 thread can sometimes be replaced by a 3 minute Skype call (Efficiency ftw).

3. *Some conversations need fewer people.* P2s are open to all. Some threads narrow to 2 people going back and forth, and they should get a room (email/Skype/ hotel). They can report back if a conclusion was reached. Other times 10 people are involved, but only 3 will do the work—not everyone's opinion has equal weight.

4. *Many conversations need to be visual.* As a rule, I never want to talk about a UI feature without a screenshot: A rough sketch explains more than 5 paragraphs of text (e.g. an idea in text may not work in pixels). All designers should be visualizers for P2 threads, saying "do you mean something like this? (show sketch)"—it improves the quality of any conversation to see, rather than just read.

5. *Thread hijacking.* This is when you carefully write a post, and then a comment comes along asking a tangential question that everyone finds more interesting. If your thread gets hijacked, start it again—don't

assume it means what you wanted to get isn't worth getting.

6. *ADD kills big ideas*. Big ideas require more thinking before commenting. Given post A (clever idea on some little thing) vs. post B (radical sweeping idea on some big thing), post A will tend to get more comments. It's easier to respond and say "cool!" or "+1." Post B requires more investment to comment, so it gets less of them. This is misleading—it suggests A is a better idea than B, when it really just means how much smaller an idea A is.

7. *How much did they read?* If someone jumps in on a thread, there's no way to know how much they read. Did they just read the previous comment? Did they read the whole thing, but not understand it? Very hard to intuit just from a comment what context they have right or wrong—I don't have a solution—ideas?

8. *Is silence acceptance?* If you post and no one comments, does that mean they read it and they agree? Read it and don't care? Or didn't read it? No way to know without poking at people. Leads should ensure all posts on their P2 are answered.

A great discussion ensued, with more than twenty comments. Comically, some of these habits were in that thread. Many comments suggested features to add to P2 to minimize these tendencies, which was inspiring and baffling. Engineering cultures always see things through feature-tinted glasses, forgetting that there are important things in the world that people, P2 users in this case, simply need to keep in mind rather than something that could ever be solved by a feature. In all, Barry's comment best reflected that my message had been heard:

I find P2 great for documenting things, ok for soliciting feedback on something, but pretty terrible for having a "discussion". If I want to discuss something with someone (or a group of people) I just ping them on IRC. Skype, phone, etc. also work for discussions. No need to have a discussion with myself on a P2.

Unlike Barry, I did like using P2s for discussions, depending on what happened. Often things went fine, but someone with a big question could take your post in a very different direction. In several frustrating debates, Evan Solomon, a programmer at the company, would leave a first comment that asked big questions. The questions were good ones, but for my purposes, the timing was frustrating. They sent the thread in a very different and, for me, useless direction. It's easy for people to dismiss a thread if the first thing they see in the comments is a long debate between two people about a detail you don't care much about. E-mail has the same vulnerability. Barry's recommendation for using other media more, and for deliberate reasons, was precisely the message I hoped to get across to everyone, and a reminder to me as well.

P2s also created special challenges for Mullenweg. Part of the growing pains for any founder is the shift from having a hand in many detailed decisions to allowing teams of people to have confident reign over their own work. As the company grew, P2s became a natural battleground, however civil, for who had what authority and how involved Matt wanted to be in the details. Even in terms of politics, there were questions: How much power did team leads have? How did team leads resolve disagreements with Matt? With each other? This was new for everyone. But unlike sitting in a meeting where you can passively observe how those situations are resolved by others, for better or worse, P2s left much to the imagination. You had to read carefully between the lines to pick up the political significance of what was going on or try to use Skype as your backchannel to find out the real story. An example was something that came to be known as "Matt bombing." This was when a team was working on something on a P2, heading in one direction. Then late in the thread, often at a point where some people felt there was already rough consensus, Matt would drop in, leave a comment advocating a different direction, and then disappear (not necessarily intentionally). Sometimes these posts were cryptic, for two reasons. First, it wasn't clear if he was merely offering an opinion for consideration or giving an order, and even if it was an order, it wasn't clear what the order was. Other times it was unclear how much of the thread he'd read or what his counterarguments were that led to his disagreement. Matt was brilliant, but it was hard to believe he had the same depth of understanding on every aspect on the thread that those on the project did.

My work style was direct by Automattic standards. I've always demanded that my bosses explain things I don't understand. I want to be taught, not told. I don't mind being proven wrong or trumped provided I learn something, but I did not follow decrees well. This makes me an excellent or frustrating person to have working for you depending on how often you like to explain yourself, as Mullenweg discovered in our occasionally long debates. Once we had a four-hour Skype argument about how a single screen should be designed, a debate that in hindsight we've agreed could have been resolved with a short voice call (yes, our debate was typed).

The countermeasure for Matt bombing is what's called "managing up." As the lead for Team Social, my job for the team was to have as few public ruffles with Matt as possible. It was my job to anticipate potential land mines with Matt, or anyone else, and resolve them proactively instead of trying to put out fires on our P2. It also meant that when Matt joined a thread and confused people, it was my job to sort it out by directly asking Matt to clarify or working as a team to respond. Managing up is essential to leadership in organizations, but it was something few others at Automattic had experience with.

For every awkward debate on a P2, there was often a private Skype chat where it was resolved. Matt set good examples for praising in public and critiquing in private. But rarely was something reported back to the P2 thread, leaving many P2 conversations with an ominous, cryptic last comment from Matt. For many employees, his comments were intimidating. It was like debating a friend on her political blog and then having the president of the United States chime in with an answer. What do you say? Most people made a polite retreat. Online it's hard to know when you've intimidated someone because silence means different things. In real life when you hurt someone's feelings, you can see it in his or her eyes and feel something in your heart. Every employee in the company, including Matt, Toni, and me, lost touch with the empathy we'd have in certain situations for people who had less authority than we did.

It would be easy to say that being distributed made this worse, but I'm not sure it did. Most companies have confusing politics about who is allowed to disagree with whom and how they're allowed to do it. However, in conventional workplaces, everyone gets to observe how their boss handles different situations and how other leaders challenge and convince them. In a regular office, you may see a great suggestion made by a colleague to your vice president and watch in horror as the underling is yelled out of the room. Or perhaps you watch how a masterful pitch was done that changed the vice president's mind, rallying you to do the same next time. If the difficult conversations are hidden in Skype, few can witness them and learn.

During my year at Automattic, no one ever yelled at me. I was never in a meeting that made me angry or want to storm out. The worst kinds of workplace moments simply weren't there. You can get only so angry at someone typing at you. People were polite, almost painfully so. But the best things about workplaces, like sharing an epiphany after working for hours at a whiteboard, were gone too. Working remotely mellowed everything out, dropping the intensity of the both the highs and the lows. Depending on your previous experience, this made things better or worse.

I did make emotional connections with my team, just as I would if I were working with them in the same building every day. But that connection was fueled and recharged by the intensity of our meet-ups. Rarely did I think our work suffered because we were working remotely. But I did have times where I thought our work would be even better if we were in the same place and time more often.

Many Automatticians, including Mullenweg, believe that distributed work is the best possible arrangement. I don't quite agree. There is personal preference involved in how people want to work and what they expect to get from it. For me, I know that for any important relationship, I'd want to be physically around that person as much as possible. If I started a rock band or a company, I'd want to share the same physical space often. The upsides outweigh the downsides. However, if the people I wanted to work with were only available remotely, I'm confident we could do great work from thousands of miles away.

CHAPTER 16

INNOVATION AND FRICTION

Jerry Hirschberg, the former head of design for Nissan, had a theory of work he called Creative Abrasion.[1] He believed you need the right amount of friction for good work to happen—not too much and not too little—and that few managers get it right. Worse, they don't know what to aim for, having never experienced a healthy creative workplace. Knowing how much friction is needed and when to apply it is the skill that successful leaders, from the coach of a competitive basketball team to the conductor of an orchestra, must master.

Many things managers do create unnecessary and unhelpful friction. From insisting on unnecessarily detailed plans, to long, stressful project review meetings, much of the boring machinery identified as management has more value for the manager's ego than the quality of work produced. Of course, if you're designing and manufacturing a nuclear-powered submarine, you need more project management rigor than if you're making a website for your friend's rock band, but few calibrate the frictions they create to the needs of the project. The only honest test of the value of any management activity is to run projects without some of them and observe how well people perform with a lighter touch. It's a test few leaders have the courage to take. The worry among managers is that this test would reveal that quality improves when they do less managing. It might just turn out that an executive whose division always demands eighty-hour workweeks might really just need a manager who knows how to hire well, put a few healthy frictions in place, and get out of the way.

Research labs and innovation groups run afoul at the other end of the spectrum: too little friction. Like a puck on an air hockey table floating around aimlessly, ideas need something to work against—a mallet or a wall—to use as leverage. There must be someone challenging ideas in ways their creators don't necessarily like in order for those creators to see the blind spots in their thinking. Breakthroughs await in those blind spots. Those critiques, delivered with the right touch, push people toward superior work. That needed friction can come from coworkers or bosses, but it has to come from somewhere. Even a cursory examination of what made the Beatles, or Xerox PARC, or the collaborators (and arguers) behind the drafting of the US Constitution, reveals a balance of friction and freedom. It's mostly in movies that tyrants get far driving creative people with a heavy hand.

Automattic is fascinating for how little built-in friction it had—or, more accurately, how much negative friction Toni Schneider and Mullenweg deliberately prevented. The ultimate friction most creative people face—the burden of meeting schedules and deadlines—was rare. There was no training around engineering estimates and prototyping methods. The few formalities, writing announcement posts and two-week cycles, weren't enforced. By early 2011, six months into my time there, few teams worked in cycles anymore. Teams returned to ad hoc planning, without much discussion about whether that shift reflected progress or regress. The saving grace at Automattic was passion. They naturally found inspiration in the world, from WordPress, or from each other. An open vacation policy had little negative impact on people who would choose to work on their own time anyway. Of course there were pockets of the company that didn't do much. The visibility of everyone's P2 posts and code check-ins made it easy for the curious to find slackers. But they were in the minority and, unlike many other workplaces, easy to work around. The negative impact of an unproductive Automattic employee was lower than at any other company I'd seen.

An example of the low friction at Automattic was what happened while we were in Athens when we decided to put Highlander, the comments project, aside. The decision took minutes. I'd told the team the day before that we might need to switch, and when the deadline came, we switched. No e-mail was sent or stakeholder consoled. There was no master schedule to update or conference calls to schedule. We simply posted the change on our P2, listed the remaining work for Highlander, and moved on. Twenty minutes later, we were hard at work on the new project, dividing up tasks on the P2 as if we'd been making switches like these together as a team for years.

The teams I worked on at Microsoft were enormous in comparison to Team Social. Of course, even a team of a thousand people is made up of many small teams, whose work is similar to any other small team's work. The difference is how much friction is inherited from the project at large. The Internet Explorer 4.0 team at its peak size during 1998 must have had 250 people. And its components were dependent on, or had dependencies from, the Windows team, an organization of thousands. On those large projects, changing tack the way Team Social did in Athens meant e-mails, phone calls, and meetings, often with rightfully angry people who had invested weeks of work based on those changes not happening. It was the consequence of using schedules, having marketing plans, and executives wrapping their reputations around projects that made all of those stressful costs around making changes unavoidable. Those annoyances were a worthy sacrifice for keeping the aircraft carrier–sized project intact, betting that when it launched, its scale and continuity would pay off in the long run against the competition. In these days of continuous deployment, grand strategies seem quaint, but for many Fortune 500 companies, it's still the way they plan their work.

Mullenweg and Schneider never worried visibly about competitors. They paid attention, as did much of the rest of the company, but it rarely had a direct impact on plans. Notes about other blogging programs appeared often on P2 threads, but the discussions rarely went deep or triggered changes. When Tumblr, a lightweight blogging tool, became a media darling in 2010, with growth numbers that any analyst would see as a threat to WordPress, not much changed at Automattic. It was common to see P2 posts referencing trendy articles proclaiming the death of blogging and articles pointing to the rise of Facebook, Twitter, and Tumblr as ending the era of blogs—articles that rarely mentioned WordPress's continued growth, as those services frequently linked to the deeper content that blogs provided.

A common move at Microsoft at moments like these was to assign someone to evaluate and report on the "tumblr threat." They'd be asked to spend a week using the competition, reading reviews, talking to customers, and writing up an analysis of what Tumblr did well that WordPress did not, and vice versa. As paranoid as Microsoft culture was with its zero sum view of the world, these reports were wise, as was pushing employees to use competitors' products and talk to their customers. I wondered what would have to happen at Automattic to earn similar attention. Open source cultures naturally see the world as positive sum, with room for everyone, but the capacity to see the world both ways is the best. Rather than just complain, at a future meet-up we experimented ourselves: Team Social used Tumblr every day for the week.

Automattic didn't invest in marketing either, certainly not in traditional forms. To do major marketing required schedules, since TV ads and magazine ad buys are purchased weeks or months in advance. Many major product launches in the world have their final schedules defined by the advertising campaign, not product development. Products can slip at low costs, but the high costs of rescheduling marketing often provide the final friction that forces shipping. Finishing in time to make the Christmas holiday season is a notorious trigger for when products release.

Continuous deployment made these downsides and benefits irrelevant. WordPress.com continually added new features, each launch creating another wave of attention generated largely by customers, the best possible advocates.

Instead of traditional marketing, WordPress.com wisely drafted behind the thriving community of WordPress itself. Natural marketing, where customers proudly promote the product themselves, is a wise strategy, as every marketer knows: it's more effective than anything marketers can do. Automattic continually invests in WordPress, from funding WordCamps to helping organize the WordPress community, but to call those efforts marketing would be cynical. As always with Mullenweg, the investment was in the long-term vibrancy of WordPress, with marketing for WordPress.com a side effect of those investments. Only a handful of teams, including VIP, Polldaddy, Akismit, and Vaultpress, had their own sales and marketing efforts. VIP had the strongest, reaching out to major companies looking for WordPress hosting and selling them high-end services. But even they did little in the way of traditional marketing since their targets were exclusive.

All combined, Automattic had a unique relationship to friction:

- No formal schedules
- Little competitive pressure
- No influence from marketers
- Minimal hierarchy/flat structure

Most people work at places with high friction from these sources and struggle to imagine working without them. There are entire jobs, like project management, based on applying friction and driving schedules. As work on Highlander and Jetpack intensified, I had to find ways to introduce friction into a culture that hadn't felt it before.

CHAPTER 17

THE INTENSE DEBATE

Before we left Athens, we managed to ship a small feature, allowing us a final celebratory dinner. It's a thrill to be in the same room at the same time when something goes live, everyone excited and worried simultaneously, each second counting down to a celebratory moment of cheering, followed by pensive investigations that nothing blew up, and then more cheering. The entire meet-up had been a series of extremes—all talk and dreams at the beginning and all work and details at the end—but it was one of the best we'd ever have.

After a meet-up, it took days for the team to re-form online. Between travel, jet lag, and catching up on the odds and ends of home life we'd left behind, little happened for the next forty-eight hours. It became an unspoken expectation: if we left a meet-up on Monday, we wouldn't find our feet again until Wednesday afternoon. Somewhere in those first days after Athens, Peatling took the liberty of updating our P2 theme. Other teams had improved their team P2s, and ours had fallen far behind. He added an image of Team Social to the header, with the bonus feature that when you moved your mouse on it, the image changed. It was a simple JavaScript trick, but at the time, P2s were simple affairs. Customizing our virtual home let us brag about our bonds online and compel other teams to respond in kind.

When we left Athens, our plan was to work on Highlander, the project to unify comments. And we'd agreed to invest a two-week cycle to make IntenseDebate, the other commenting project, more reliable. Those two weeks flew by, and all I had to show was a report on why we'd made little progress. Only Beau was familiar with IntenseDebate, but even he was working on unfamiliar parts. Adams and Peatling had limited progress. Everyone had the same opinion: "We're disappointed, making slow, steady progress, and can turn the corner soon." There were no alarm bells or roadblocks. Was this good or bad?

This is a classic management situation. What can you do? There are only a handful of choices:

1. *Look at it myself.* If I were more of a programmer, I could have jumped in. The bet would be I could see something that they didn't. That's a big bet, though, and possibly seen as a lack of trust.
2. *Ask another programmer to look.* This is the same as the first option through delegation.
3. *Change something.* Making the project simpler might help. I could sharpen the goal, ask better questions, or simplify the scenario. I asked Adams if he saw a way, but he didn't. The smallest useful goal was the one we had.
4. *Kill the project.* Give up and move on.
5. *Keep going.* Assume everything is fine, and we just need more time.

I went with #5. We put in another week. I gave everyone more attention, switching from IRC to Skype for the equivalent of office drop-by chats. I poked at the ultimate questions for managers:

- Do I know everything I need to know?
- Do they trust me enough to tell me things they think I don't want to hear?

There was only one way to find out. Every few days I gently inquired about where things were at, what the next steps were, if they were blocked and how I could help. Although these chats revealed little, they did clarify what was on my mind to them. It also opened a private Skype backchannel with everyone, something I hadn't done before. The chats with Adams proved most useful. He seemed to have the broadest perspective in his responses. But even he saw no silver bullet and didn't expect to see one either. In a company dominated by incrementalism, this project challenged my team in unfamiliar ways. We had made a big bet that was hard to divide into small pieces.

The lingo for the challenge is what's called *refactoring*. The word is a fancy way of saying you're going to take the guts of something one part at a time and rework it without disturbing the rest. I don't like the word because many people who use it confuse words with reality: simply because you have a fancy word for something doesn't make you any smarter. It probably makes you stupider because you confuse your precise vocabulary with precise skills. The problem with problem-solving methods, which all business methodologies are, is that they are abstractions, but the world is not abstract. Real work contains hard parts that no method can dictate for you. No method can capture how and when to abandon the method or tweak it; only a team and its leader can do that. And for a team to do that successfully, they need to trust each other. Too often teams are imprisoned by methodologies when they should be empowered by them (a sentiment captured in the Manifesto for Agile Software Development, a set of simple principles for making software[1]). Methodologies are often another bad friction that managers impose, putting more faith in a bunch of rules than in the people they've hired. I'd take a great team with bad methods over a lousy team with great methods any day.

As we made our way through December with little progress on IntenseDebate, I pulled another trick from my hat: increase motivation. We were excited about Highlander and Jetpack, and defining those projects might inspire us to push through the IntenseDebate work. I flew down to San Francisco to meet with Beau and Adams: an experimental mini-team meet-up. Would some face time help us turn the corner or have no impact? There was only one way to know.

Beau let us in at Automattic headquarters, and we had the place to ourselves. We were told there was a whiteboard somewhere in the office, but it took a half-hour to find it, an indicator of how rarely the office was used. When we found it, the markers were missing, which led to more searching. We looked through the shelves behind the bar, where rumor had it that basic office supplies were stashed and found a single blue pen but no eraser. Automattic had great tools for remote work, but working in person at headquarters was like being stranded on a desert island. Yet it made us laugh, which always helps, and we got to work.

Peatling was in Ireland, and we looped him in on IRC. But to kick off the meeting, we started another team joke: whoever comes last to a meeting is assigned all the work no one wants to do. Since Peatling wasn't coming, he was technically infinitely late. Our first act of work was to list Jetpack as a single work item and put his name next to it, which we also posted on the P2 for him to see.

Clarity again is key for starting projects. I arrived with three things we needed to make:

1. A map of work divided roughly into two-week chunks
2. A sensible order for working on the chunks
3. One map for Highlander and one for Jetpack, noting where they shared work

The fact that I wasn't a programmer made this more effective. Beau and Adams, and not the lead, would have to make the map. I was free to play to role of asker of questions, both dumb and insightful ones: both kinds would force explanations of assumptions, revealing hidden challenges. In a few hours, we'd mapped out a year or more of work that would deliver Highlander and Jetpack to the world. We posted it on the P2 with an invitation for feedback from others in the company. Finally we had something to show that people could comment on for what had been a long-standing piece of vaporware. Plans aren't code, that's for sure, but it was one big step forward.

CHAPTER 18

FOLLOW THE SUN

Do you know what the worst possible way to distribute a team on a planet is? We found out. In late December 2010, Beau moved back to Perth, Australia. Team Social became the most distributed team in the company, despite our small size, with each employee eight hours apart from another. Mike and I were on Pacific Standard Time, Andy was +8, and Beau was now +16. I foolishly tried to use a meeting calendar to see what our meeting time options were and plugged in different options again and again. I thought there was something wrong with the tool because every time I tried a new combination, someone would have to be up at 2:00 a.m. Finally it dawned on me that my team had hit the natural limits of space and time on planet Earth. For us to speak at the same time, someone would have to be miserable. Beau graciously volunteered. The plan was that while Mike and I attended at the regular 10:00 a.m. slot, Andy would tune in at 6:00 p.m. from Ireland (the time slot he'd had for weeks), and Beau would have to go to bed, then wake up at 2:00 a.m. to join in.

Each week part of the early entertainment was joking to see if Beau would make it at all and how cranky he'd be:

9:58: *beaulebens:* OMG, I'm awake
9:59: *apeatling:* woooo
10:00: *berkun:* and you're here before mdawaffe [Adams]
10:01: *apeatling:* did you actually go to sleep?

10:01: <mdawaffe has joined #social>:
10:02: *berkun:* we now have complete team social voltron status
10:02: *berkun:* although I think voltron had 5
10:02: *mdawaffe:* socialcats, HO!
10:02: *beaulebens:* I went to sleep, and then woke up
10:03: *beaulebens:* we have all corners of the globe covered now
10:03: *apeatling:* we should be team globepsan

Over the weeks this near sci-fi time travel degree of separation increased the drag on team morale. No matter what technologies you use, when half the team is waking up while the other half is going to bed, things will feel weird, at least at first.

Had I planned better for Beau's move, we'd have changed work assignments. Years ago I had a team of programmers in India working on Internet Explorer. In what's called Follow The Sun, they worked the night shift while my team in Redmond worked days. If I planned well, we'd find magic in going to bed frustrated by a missing puzzle piece, and waking to find it in our in-box. It was like having a friend in the future. (Of course, workers at factories around the world have rotated in shifts for centuries, so the idea itself wasn't novel.) But the IntenseDebate work wasn't divided in a way that made this easy. When we started, we'd done the simplest and, in hindsight, laziest system, dividing the work into parts each programmer could work on independently. As a young team, this was a mistake, a mistake that was mine. Thinking the project was simply a two-week maintenance task, I didn't see the downsides to having everyone work alone. But by the beginning of 2011, we'd been working on it for nearly two months, yet I hadn't thought to redivide the work.

December would be the least productive month in Team Social's entire history. The work on IntenseDebate slogged on, repeating the same cycle of little progress, low excitement, slow learning, and promises for a turned corner. Each week I'd consider the same sunk cost choices listed in the previous chapter. The rule for sunk cost is never to allow the past to drive the present, and I didn't. I wasn't trying to salvage the previous week's work. Instead I took each week on its own, weighed my options in the present, and continued to invest. Each week I'd talk with everyone one-on-one to see if there was some new insight and to hunt for hints at what I could do as lead to help us turn corners. I mixed in other small projects, one- or two-day efforts for each, to give them something to ship and take a break. These snack projects prevented our team from going dark in output and gave us sparks of morale. Our load of bug fixes was constant too, but none of it broke us out of our slump. Before we knew it, the winter holidays were almost upon us, and we were still stuck on the same project. In retrospect, I don't see the wider distribution of our team as the cause for our poor productivity. Instead, it was the division of labor and the low morale for IntenseDebate. When our team became more dispersed, I had the choice of switching to a simpler project and have them all work together, a good choice when learning something new. But we'd already put the Highlander project aside. I didn't want to put the IntenseDebate work on the shelf as well, as we'd then have two major mothballed projects hanging over us. Instead I continued to bet on patience and for one of my guys to break through.

Adams was the first to launch something major for IntenseDebate, a rebuilt sync engine that addressed the most fragile part of how IntenseDebate worked. There was much rejoicing, certainly by me: finally a ray of light. Often the first step, the first undeniable sign of progress, is the hardest to get. With the first win under your belt, everyone has a clear reminder that wins are possible. Programmers are competitive by nature, and someone has to set the pace on every team, constantly demonstrating what can be done. In that first fall and winter, that lead horse was Adams. On a team that has good morale, seeing teammates launch things inspires, and inspiration brings with it new effort and ideas. Of course, Adams's launch shook the code tree and new bugs fell. But we fixed them quickly, and as their count diminished, it was clear they were the fallout of the improvement, not signs of a setback.

It's a hidden, and often scary, cost of rebuilding something: even a perfect improvement reveals old issues hidden by the mistakes of the past. Like making that first clean spot on an old, dusty window, your first sweep of improvements opens your eyes to things you should have noticed long ago.

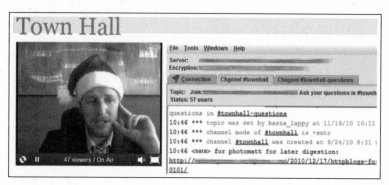

All across Automattic, things slowed down for the holidays, just as they do at most other companies around the world. Mullenweg was fond of holiday spirit in his way, and at the town hall meeting in late December, he donned a Santa hat. He also turned on a snowflake effect to be added to various WordPress.com pages, another hint at the personality of the company coming out through the product itself. Despite millions of blogs and all of WordPress's success, there was still silliness, a humanity, that Mullenweg made sure we and our customers didn't forget. These efforts were corny, but they had positive effects that were hard to measure. Reminders to have a sense of humor gave us room for trying ideas to improve WordPress.com that'd we never pursue in a company afraid to behave in public like a person instead of a machine.

CHAPTER 19

THE RISE OF JETPACK

arly in 2011, Mullenweg and I discussed launching Jetpack at SXSW, one of the biggest media events in the world. Automattic rarely did product launches, but I was familiar with them and the work required to do them well. SXSW was in March and the timing just might work, we thought. My biggest concern wasn't the time line: it was the collision of Automattic's culture with a hard public deadline. We discussed it as a team and committed to deliver Jetpack in time for SXSW, which started on March 13, 2011.

I was excited, which surprised me. Half of what makes managing projects tough is deadlines, and it felt good to awaken a large part of my team leader brain—the bundle of neurons trained in how to ship things on time. The additional challenge for my team was that Jetpack would be a plug-in that people would download. It was not code that ran live on WordPress.com servers, meaning that any bug fixes would require a new release of the software. If on March 14 we discovered that Jetpack had a horrible bug, we'd have to rerelease and ask everyone to download again, something embarrassing and painful, especially for a new product.

In all, five warning bells went off in my mind:

1. *Success demanded a different culture*. If we missed the date, Automattic would look bad and Jetpack's launch would fail. I imagined Mullenweg up on stage doing magic tricks in front of a huge crowd, killing time instead of announcing Jetpack to the world.

2. *Programmers would have to do estimates.* I hadn't seen a single work estimate at Automattic. You can't be on time unless you estimate work. The first time that a team that has never done estimates before does them, accuracy is poor, as is how much they care about the consequences.

3. *We'd need more people on the team.* The rough work map we made for Jetpack implied that three programmers was not enough.[1]

4. *Jetpack needed a simple user interface.* Jetpack was a bridge for various blogging features. The technology required to do this was complex, but users' experiences had to be as simple as flipping a switch and forgetting it was there.

5. *We'd need release management and compatibility testing.* Web programmers work with browser compatibility all the time, but Jetpack worked on different servers. We'd need to test Jetpack on many different hosts. This meant another unfamiliar bag of tricks: bug tracking, test plans, and release candidates (RC), things rarely used at Automattic.

Mullenweg clarified the importance of the project, and as a good leader should, he offered whatever resources I needed. It's a great bullshit test of any boss who says, "X is important." If she doesn't match that statement with resources, she's incompetent, insincere, or both. If it's important, prove it. Importance is always relative to other projects, not verbal fairy dust to sprinkle over your staff. Team Social borrowed two people, both from Team Data. Joen Asmussen was a sharp young designer living in Denmark. Also joining was Andy Skelton, based in Texas, one of the first employees at Automattic. He worked on Stats, the most popular WordPress plug-in in the world. Much of the work for Jetpack would be to rebuild Stats to use the plumbing provided by Jetpack. I hadn't worked with either Asmussen or Skelton, but I was betting on Team Social to make it easy for them to fit in.

Thanks to serendipity, we had a great start. Adams finished his InternalDebate work and immediately began scouting Jetpack. He took the road map we'd made in San Francisco and broke it down into six task lists, an amazing burst of organizational production for an Automattician. He understood what I needed: I didn't care about estimates but needed another level of granularity in lists to help us decide next steps. I was always pushing for lists of things and putting them in order, like good project managers do. I did care about the lists themselves, but early in a project, I cared more about the thinking Adams was forced to do in order to generate the lists.

There were two missions clear in my mind:

- Ensure simplicity.
- Plan the project to be easily managed.

The natural mistake engineers make is to build from the bottom up. They leave the user interface last, assuming it is the least complex technology. This is wrong. Humans are much more complex than software, and since the interface has to interact with people, it's the most difficult to do well. By building from the bottom up, technologists paint themselves into a corner, resulting in ugly, hard-to-use things. By the time they finally got to the user interface work, so many constraints exist that even the best designers in the world couldn't salvage the project. The answer is simple: design the user interface first. This is a mandate at any organization that makes things people love to use.

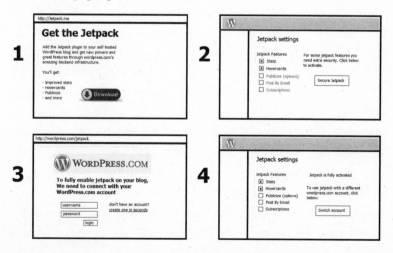

I sketched the first designs, and marked each screen with a letter or number for easy reference in conversation. The goal of these mock-ups was to force simplicity. I was happy to see questions and critiques provided they pointed us to making the design simpler. Even if my ideas were hated, it'd be fine if I succeeded in implanting in everyone's brain the central ambition of a streamlined customer's experience. A long P2 thread began with questions, ideas, clarifications, and more, all following the intended spirit. We were on track with mission A.

For mission B, plan the project, I needed a special list. The easiest way to work to a schedule is a spreadsheet with three things:

- Each work item, listed in priority
- The developer assigned
- The developer's work estimate

You can never take a schedule seriously unless it has all three of these. It's only when people see their names on the board next to a promise they've made that a schedule is real. I was confident Team Social would at least try to work this way, but would we stick to it? Making a schedule is one thing, but following it is another. On January 15, 2011, Team Social had its first voice meeting in history, and Andy Skelton and Joen joined in from around the world. Other teams had experimented with voice, which always made sense to me, but until now, there was no motivating factor to switch. A new project is an easy opportunity to do an experiment or two. It went so well that we never used IRC for meetings again.

The meeting went well, and morale was high. Everyone improved Adams's lists and worked with me to divide tasks into priority 1 (must have) and priority 2 (might be nice) items. I kept priority 1 as lean as possible. I took these lists over to a Google Doc spreadsheet, and for the remainder of the project, it was our scoreboard for how we were doing.

The problem is that spreadsheets quickly get out of date, especially if the team is productive. Typically managers spend hours tending schedules, and I expected I'd have to do the same. The pleasant surprise was that my team regularly tended to their items. It was a project management miracle. At each Monday meeting, we'd open the spreadsheet together for a quick review, talking over Skype while looking at the same screen, making sure everything was up to date. These meetings provided much entertainment since we all had our own cursor in Google Docs and could type in obnoxious things in other people's work items while someone else was talking.

	Area	Task	Estimate (days)	Priority	Automattician	Done?
	Project Jetpack	**Complete Task List**				
9	Server	Sign user up for a mailing list during 2nd stage of connection	3	1	beaulebens	
10	Server	Management UI for viewing/removing a user's connections (for users and site_admins())	3	1	apeatling	1
11	Server	New XML-RPC method: JetPack.testConnection	1	1	beaulebens	
12	Server	Check nonces from signed .ORG -> .COM requests. New memcache group/bucket? We only need to store the data for about one minute.	1	1	beaulebens	
13	Server	add user to blog()/remove user from blog()	1	1	mdawaffe	1
14	Client	3a. Registration failures. Message and button to try again (instead of deactivate/reactivate)?	3	1	apeatling	
15	Client	3b. OAuth user flow errors (all the current wp_die()s).	3	1	mdawaffe	1
16	Client	3c. OAuth user flow error=access_denied (user opted out).	1	1	mdawaffe	1
17	Client	8a. Main admin screen UI	3	1		
18	Client	8c. Post-installation notice/error UI	1	1		
19	Client	8c. plugin_action_links to point to main admin screen UI	1	1	mdawaffe	1
20	Client	8d. Do we want a disable/enable UI?	3	1		
21	Client	9. Get the plugin working when the blog has ugly permalinks (/jetpack.verify/ not working)	3	1	mdawaffe	1
22	Hovercards		1	1		
23	Shortcodes		1	1		
24		1. Allow authorization with X_JETPACK				

Joen took over sketching duties and masterfully represented our decisions, pulled from P2 discussions, into his designs. He was a star: unlike designers who shy away from the mess of engineering constraints, he did what the best designers do: he drove issues to resolution. And he did it with no ego, caring only about progress rather than credit. I couldn't have chosen a better designer for the challenges of Jetpack.

To build Jetpack demanded that Beau and Adams figure out a spaghetti-like mess of security, authentication, and cross-domain issues. There were good reasons no one had taken on this project before despite how long it had been talked about: it was complex and scary. This had implications for the user interface, and as questions from Adams and Beau arose, simple mock-ups weren't sufficient to capture the intricate decisions we had to make. Joen made a flowchart capturing the unresolved issues in the user flow and related engineering, revising it over time. This condensation of thinking into a diagram was enormously valuable. In a regular office, this would have been sprawled across a whiteboard, but he'd replicated the same effect even though we were working remotely.

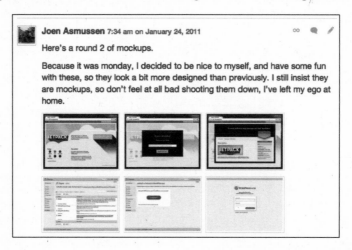

Jetpack was off to an excellent start. But as the SXSW March deadline neared, it was clear we'd need to work full time on Jetpack while at our next team meet-up, planned for New York City in February. Mullenweg would be in town, so we planned to show him what we had and get feedback. Also joining us in New York was the first new member of Team Social: Hugo Baeta, a designer from Lisbon, Portugal.

Hugo had passed the hire-by-trial process, but the leads were always consulted when it came to placing people on teams. Matt Thomas, the creative director for the company, ran most design trials. When Hugo passed, he reached out to me to see if I thought Hugo would be a fit. Inspired by the success of our audio team meetings, I talked to Hugo on voice. He told me I was the first Automattician's voice he'd heard, which I thought was both funny and sad. We talked for an hour, and mostly I asked him to tell me what he thought was wrong with WordPress.com. I'd seen his portfolio and he passed Matt Thomas's bar, so I wasn't concerned much about his ability. But I needed to check him for attitudes: good designers are never happy. They always see ways to improve what they've done. He passed my test and finished his support tour just in time to meet us in New York.

Wanting to avoid the mistakes of the Athens venue, I found a large apartment in SoHo in Lower Manhattan, with good wi-fi and plenty of space. Unlike Athens, we were hard at work from the first night we arrived, building on the good momentum we'd had working remotely. The first night, we found a neighborhood Italian restaurant, Bianca, just around the corner. One afternoon we took a break and walked down to my favorite building in the world, the Brooklyn Bridge, a fitting inspiration for Jetpack: connect things. We walked back through Chinatown, stopping for team pictures at the silliest places we could find.

The next day we worked hard to do a .5 release of Jetpack, a private alpha release. We invited all the Automatticians and friends in the WordPress community to try it out and report bugs to us. Mullenweg reviewed our work and was pleased. While he was in our apartment, he broadcast his town hall meeting to the company and had us participate. It's a strange thing to stare at a webcam knowing all of the coworkers you know mostly through text, were watching. We were all uncomfortable sitting there on a couch, staring into the little red eye of a camera, except for Matt, who had been doing these for months. The highlight was the use of an old song to close the town hall meeting. During the week, my team swapped videos of old *Schoolhouse Rock* and *Sesame Street* videos on YouTube, and the Pointer Sisters' rendition of what's called The Pinball Number Count was the earworm, the tune you can't get out of your mind, of the week.[2] Matt played it for the company at the end of the meeting, which made me laugh and feel not so old. If nothing else, I could make sure those good memes lived on.

On our last night I arranged for a big dinner, something I hoped to make a team tradition—a chance to wrap up the trip with a long, relaxing meal and to talk about what had gone well and what could have been better. We went to NY Prime, an over-the-top steakhouse that we found endlessly entertaining, for its clichés of enormous portions, prom dates, and fork-laden dining formalities. Largely we talked about IntenseDebate and made a list of how we'd have managed the project differently, as well as what we'd learned. I wrote up the list later and posted it on the P2. I rarely saw postmortems at Automattic, and although I posted ours for our benefit, I was hoping to set an example for others. A year in the future someone might wonder how or why we'd done what we did, and a good postmortem captures wisdom you never find in code.

With our serious obligations complete, my last mission while in New York was to add to the company tradition called "blank in a blank": a P2 of pictures by Automatticians who had taken photos where something was inside something else. The most famous photo was Hanni inside an oven. The Theme Team had a photo with all members standing inside a phone booth. As our dinner wound down, we decided our best idea was to take a photo at the iconic clock in the center of Grand Central station, a mile or more away. It was 1:00 a.m., and the prospect of getting there before it closed was slim, which led to another idea: lets take a limousine to get there. Worst case, we'd have a picture of Team Social in a limo. Having no idea how to procure a limo yet responsible as the leader of these shenanigans, I asked the hostess of the restaurant, Mandi Nadel. She thought we were funny, perhaps in a pathetic sort of way. While we stood at the hostess table in the restaurant entrance, she spent the next twenty-five minutes calling limo services. Each one refused to come out so late, even for a short trip. Time was running out: when Grand Central closed down, there was no backup plan. Finally, after asking her boss and coworkers, she found us a driver who would do it. When he arrived at 1:30 a.m., we jumped in and took a photo. (We also sent Mandi a big box of WordPress shwag as a thank-you.)

On return to our home towns, the pace continued. We continued to do small releases, arriving at .9 with two weeks to go. We switched to meeting daily, even if just for five minutes. We'd review all the open issues, who was working on what, and any adjustments needed. Adams put together a simple test plan with steps to use on each major host and a new list of hosting companies and who was responsible for testing on them. Mullenweg convinced Bluehost, DreamHost, GoDaddy, HostGator, Media Temple, and Network Solutions to include Jetpack in new downloads of WordPress from their services. When SXSW came along, we were ready. We had several days without new issues or new fixes needed, making for a smooth runway to unveil Jetpack to the world.

The SXSW launch went smoothly.[3] Mullenweg's slot on stage was an interview rather than a dedicated product launch, but it worked well. Team Social had made bets on how many downloads we'd see that first day, and we were all much too optimistic: there were just a few thousand—a good number but we'd expected many more. For the next months, our team continually added new features to Jetpack. The plug-in formed a bridge between WordPress.com's servers and WordPress, but that bridge was useful for bloggers only if it brought features they needed across it. Soon we released 1.2 and 1.3, releases occurring every few weeks, and helped other teams launch Jetpack features too. As of this writing, Jetpack has been downloaded over 5 million times, making it one of the most popular WordPress plug-ins in history.

Soon after the Jetpack launch, our team photo from Grand Central appeared on our P2, along with a new name for our organization. With Jetpack, Highlander, and other features we'd made, we always seemed to be consolidating and unifying things and making rules for others to follow: we were socialists! And like any good socialist organization, we should be labeled a bureau.

Thus, we dubbed ourselves the Bureau of Socialization. Adams's first P2 design with the hammer and sickle had been prescient. The new name would end up being more than a joke and even outlast me on the team.

CHAPTER 20

SHOW ME THE MONEY

How WordPress.com made money was a question I was often asked when I spoke at events. The very popularity of WordPress made these explanations complicated. The distinction among the three entities of WordPress (the open source project), WordPress.com (one use of WordPress), and Automattic, Inc. (the company behind WordPress.com) caused constant confusion. Well-known brands are monolithic: Disney is Disney, Coke is Coke. They rarely divide their intellectual property or agenda into externally visible factions (they keep the joys of infighting inside if they can). The price of the WordPress project's independence from any corporation was a public relations challenge WordPress.com would continually face.

How WordPress.com makes money is simple and, much like the strategy of the company, transparent: the business works on the freemium model, where the core product is free to everyone. But there are four streams of revenue that make it work:

1. *Upgrades*. For users who want more storage space, a premium theme, or their own domain name, WordPress.com sells them for a small subscription fee. By giving many features for free, it doesn't need a sales team because the product sells itself.
2. *Advertising*. If you count all the blogs on WordPress.com, the total traffic for WordPress.com makes it the fifteenth most trafficked website in the world. A small amount, less than 1

percent, of visited pages have ads displayed on them, and they generate revenue. One upgrade available for users is to pay for no ads, but few pages have ads, making it an unpopular upgrade.

3. *VIP*. Premier companies like CNN, *Time* magazine, CBS, and NBC Sports host their websites on WordPress.com servers. They pay a premium price to get the benefits of one of the best server infrastructures in the world and support from a special team of engineers (Team VIP).

4. *Partnerships*. WordPress.com sometimes does partnership deals with other services.

By the time, I was hired, all of these were in place but got little public attention, fueling curiosity about the business. Most companies sell their products hard, but at least that ensures their customers know they have something to sell. In WordPress.com's case, it was easy to think the service was run by volunteers. One running joke I had with Andy Peatling was about the visibility, or invisibility, of the WordPress.com store: as a happy customer with money to throw at WordPress.com, you'd have to look long and hard to figure out where to throw it. Many web services hit you over the head with upgrades. By contrast, the only way to get to the WordPress.com store is a small text button that says "Store," tucked inside a long list on the left edge of the dashboard.

Of the many P2s at the company, one was called Money. It was a quiet place. Since there was no team dedicated to the store or to revenue, it was no one's primary job to actively work on it. One side effect of having teams is there will always be things that fall through the cracks. Teams create territories. This is a force for good since it helps people focus and feel pride. But it creates problems for projects that fall between teams. If you try to cover everything, the teams are unfocused, and if you cover too little, there's no room for growth. But even if you carefully design teams, the turf needs to be conceptual, not territorial. Organizations become bureaucratic as soon as people define their job around a specific rule, or feature, rather than a goal. For example, if you tell me my job is to cook the french fries, I will resist anything that threatens the existence of french fries, since when they go away, so does my job. But if you tell me my job is to make side dishes for customers, I'll be open to changing from fries to onion rings or other side dishes, even ones we've yet to invent, since my identity isn't tied to a particular side dish but instead to the role side dishes play. Bureaucracies form when people's jobs are tied strictly to rules and procedures rather than the effect those things are supposed to have on the world. At the time, I thought the fact that upgrades were hard to find was madness, but it was madness I respected. There were clear priorities implied by how the teams had been chosen. There was no Team Revenue by design.

Back at the Seaside meet-up I'd talked to Schneider about my observations. When I brought up revenue and the hard-to-find store, he laughed knowingly, as he often did. He had a calm, charming way about him. He was easy to talk to about just about anything, and as a leader, he reached one of the highest bars in that he practiced what he preached. He was born in Switzerland and had come to the United States to study computer science at Stanford, working for various tech companies before finding his way to Automattic.

As one of the few people at Automattic with experience at many companies, he shared how the cultural aversion to revenue was something he'd noticed too. He explained that the cultural history of WordPress wasn't filled with entrepreneurs or veterans of big businesses. It was mostly self-employed WordPress developers and designers for whom working at Automattic was their first experience at a "major" corporation. They didn't bring the normal expectations of people who had worked for years at established companies. Many had contributed to WordPress for free, expecting nothing in return. The decisions for what teams should exist and what goals they should have weren't taken lightly. Schneider and Mullenweg met every few weeks at NOVA, a small bar tucked into the SOMA neighborhood of San Francisco. They'd review major projects and adjust priorities for the company. This might have meant asking a team to start a project or forming a new team. The store had been identified as important, but it didn't rank high enough to earn resources. They were willing to wait to invest in the store as the company was breaking even or better, because the store would require a big investment to do well. Team Social was created during one of these planning meetings to address the clear demand for WordPress.com to help bloggers engage with their audiences and social networks.

Mullenweg had fantastic restraint about the drive for profits. He'd seen many founders make the mistake of chasing revenue too early and too fast. He imagined many ways to make revenue growth a natural part of the design of WordPress.com, but in good time. During my year there, they chose targeted investments, like adding paid domain registrations to the steps of signing up for a new blog. Despite the alarm bells in my brain over leaving easy revenue on the table, I respected the conviction for patience. I've met few executives with similar faith and patience for the long-term prospects of what they were doing.

I had the chance to speak once at the Automattic board of directors meeting. Having presented to executives many times, I peppered Mullenweg with questions for how to prepare. As was typical, he found my procedural concerns amusing. He told me I didn't need any slides ("We haven't had a slide deck in years," was what he typed over Skype). I told Mullenweg I'd give a rundown of what Team Social's goals were and what we were working on, which he thought was fine. I was dubious this was sufficient, but knowing Mullenweg would be there if things went off the rails, I'd at least be able to shake my fist at him.

In attendance were Mullenweg, Schneider, Mike Hirshland (a veteran venture capitalist), Phillip Black (a founder of True Ventures), Tony Conrad (founder of True Ventures), and Anne Dorman (Automattic's chief financial officer). Although they grilled me on questions about my team and our goals, it was the most straightforward and low-key meeting with executives and venture capitalists I'd had. Mullenweg didn't say much, as everything I'd said he'd heard before. My read of the room was that Mullenweg was in great standing: he had little to prove, and there was nothing of contention on the table. Or perhaps they'd wisely covered the fun conversations before I arrived. I'd never chat with the board again about my team's work. They seemed just as comfortable staying out of the way of employees as Schneider and Mullenweg did.

My explanation for everything I'd experienced in the business of Automattic, including the dreamy meeting with the board, was the story of WordPress.com's amazing growth. Its traffic charts were something that entrepreneurs fanaticize about. The traffic across WordPress.com had long been in the top twenty in the world, and had been growing annually at a steady pace. This meant that opportunities were tremendous for all of the revenue sources I've described. Even if the rate of growth slowed, it was still one of the most valuable properties in the history of the web. Even as far back as 2007, Automattic turned down an acquisition offer for $200 million.[1] Many understood the proven potential of what they had built and planned to build.

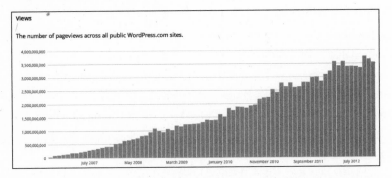

The longer I worked at the company, the more I wondered about the behind-the-scenes story for this tremendous growth. Clearly the balance of it was following the growth of WordPress itself. As more of the web used WordPress, WordPress.com followed along like a race car drafting behind the leader. Anyone who'd heard good things about WordPress could try WordPress.com before trying to set up something on their own server. But the more I studied how that growth developed, one name, and team, kept coming up: Raanan Bar-Cohen and the VIP team. They were the connection between Automattic and premier companies. They counted for a large chunk of that traffic and gave tremendous brand recognition to WordPress.com.

The first striking thing about Raanan was that he never seemed to sleep. I didn't understand if there were two or more of him who worked in shifts or if his genetics allowed him to work at twice normal speed, but he seemed to know what was going on everywhere, all the time. I don't mean just within Automattic, but across the web and publishing worlds. Much like Mullenweg and Barry Abrahamson, Raanan should be studied by scientists to understand their capacity for information consumption: they all calmly filtered, processed, and responded to more information than anyone else I'd seen at the company, and with unusual clarity and grace (at least from my end; working remotely, I had no sense of how well they balanced their daily lives). But awareness wasn't the most interesting thing about Raanan. It was how he embodied many of the experiences and attitudes Automattic needed but didn't have. Most employees' personal networks were tightly wound around WordPress. While Mullenweg's and Schneider's industry connections were excellent, the rest of the company's were poor. Raanan heavily tipped the balance toward the favorable.

The role of business development, one of Raanan's roles, is an odd one. It falls between both technology and business, and sales and marketing. Bizdev (as they're often called) folks are paid to make connections with other businesses, which could be for sales, partnerships, information, acquisitions, or anything in between. It's hard to take some of these people seriously, since, like salesmen, it's easy for them to be too pushy, phony, or stupid. It's easy to find people in this role at successful companies who in just ten minutes will clearly fall into two or more of those failings. But even those who are too pushy or phony can play a vital role: their network creates opportunities a young company needs to survive. It's a critical job, even when it's not done well. Provided these people have a good network, can pitch well, and close decent deals, they earn their pay. But great ones are rare.

In my time at Automattic, I found Raanan to be persistent, authentic, and brilliant. While managing Team VIP, he reached out to teams with reports on other companies as well as feedback on the team's own plans. His savvy went beyond business development and into my expertise of design and product planning. Like Andy Peatling, Raanan was capable of starting his own company. Both had diverse skills that could, like Mullenweg had, successfully lead their own ship. And that was part of the magic of Automattic: Raanan loved what he was doing. He'd joined in part because of the mission to democratize publishing. He'd worked at Time, Inc. & Dow Jones, advocating the use of WordPress while he worked there. Impressed by Matt, Toni, and Barry and intrigued by the idea of working remotely, he joined in 2008. I didn't work with Raanan directly much, which was a shame. Mostly he'd make suggestions on Team Social's P2, but as good as many were, they landed in our backlog more often than not.

Like Raanan, I understood why many employees were so happy at the company. It was a dream job to work for a company that made something they loved, in the same way some children dream of working for Disney, NASA, or the New York Knicks. For others, it was the fact that they could join a premier company without having to relocate. They loved where they lived or had family obligations preventing change, and this was a rare chance to work for a premier company. But for more established veterans like Raanan, Barry, and a handful of others, it was the entire package. The deal at Automattic was centered on quality of life, not just the quality of life while at work.

The last surprise about money was how rarely financial compensation came up. Unlike most companies, this was never a frequent topic of conversation. It's hard to explain, but raises and bonuses simply weren't as central to how people thought about their jobs. Most organizations have so much tension about financial rewards that they create an elaborate system of performance reviews. The result is another data trap: the more complex performance reviews become, the less effective they are. In most organizations, people wonder when someone pushed a project that wasn't good, or was too critical of one that was, whether they were gaming for a promotion or a raise. I never felt that way at Automattic, even with the people who worked for me on my team.

Mullenweg and Schneider had an implicit policy of not having many policies about raises or compensation. They really did not want it to be the focal point for thinking about what people got from the company, and it wasn't. They paid at- or above-market salaries, and for the majority of employees, it was the highest-paying job they'd ever had. The distributed nature of the company was never a bargaining plan: the costs of sending employees to team meet-ups balanced out any financial advantages of remote work. But regardless of finances, Automatticians recognized they had more freedom over their time than the rest of the working world, perhaps the most important compensation there is. They call the rate at which people leave a company the attrition rate. It's a fantastic way to examine the health of an organization. In the eighteen months I worked there, fewer than six people left, a very low number.

By comparison, the turnover rate in Silicon Valley is likely higher than anywhere else in the world, since the demand for talent is so high. Many of Automattic's employees, although talented, work in places where there's less demand and fewer high-profile companies to choose from. To leave Automattic means either returning to self-employment or relocation, things they took the job at Automattic to avoid. This is a trap of a kind: complaints that might motivate an employee to switch companies in a major city have to be tolerated if you work remotely in a small town, since there are few alternatives. In the end, every executive judges the organization by who leaves and who stays. Employees can yell and complain, but there is no louder message to management that something is wrong than forcing them to watch a great employee walk out the door.

CHAPTER 21

PORTLAND AND THE COLLECTIVE

I remember as a kid in Queens, New York, finding ant nests under parts of the sidewalk. I'd use all the might I could muster in my small hands to pull up cracked stones just to look inside. I was amazed to see hundreds of ants swirling in organized chaos, all working independently yet also together. I could never understand how the ants, which individually seemed so dumb, could do the amazing acts of engineering and logistics to build and supply their colonies. I naturally assumed the ant queen, wherever she was, must have been the brains of the whole show, but this is wrong. Her brain isn't any smarter than any other ant. She gives no orders and makes no plans. Instead the intelligent behavior emerges out of the collective choices all of the ants make. It's foreign to us, and our faith in hierarchies, but science bears out emergent intelligence as fact. If the conditions are right, a community can be much more than the sum of its parts.[1]

I often found myself going to Automattic's master P2 list, scrolling through to see what my colleagues were up to, for similar reasons that I enjoyed watching ants. Like watching schools of fish or flocks of birds move, it was as if everyone's brain was tuned to a certain radio signal, calmly chipping away at what needed to be done. It was inspiring how at nearly any time of day, people in this collective, living in various places around the world, were working in a kind of harmony. They weren't automatons like ants, mindlessly following along, but they did choose to apply their intelligence to something much larger than themselves. I rarely tired of watching that list scroll by, and I miss watching it even now. But as mesmerizing as it was, there were some challenges at Automattic the collective failed to overcome. I've mentioned before that parts of WordPress itself were not designed well, and WordPress.com inherited them. Most users found WordPress easy to use, but only after they overcame a medium-sized learning curve. WordPress was filled with layers of distracting complexity, a classic symptom of engineer-led design. Many of these layers helped WordPress's soaring rise in popularity, but that rise was predicated on appealing to programmers and organizations with technical demands, a different ambition from achieving simplicity for bloggers themselves.

Most designers at Automattic, the people I'd expect to lead in improving the holistic design of WordPress, kept their heads down. Many designers by their nature dislike conflict. Although they often have bold ideas, they struggle to find the courage to fight for those ideas. In a culture that emphasized camaraderie and sharing work, it was simply easier for designers, and everyone else, to avoid tough problems like ease of use and stick to the safety of fixing bugs or adding new features, even though new features contributed to the decline of simplicity.

One visible example of WordPress's accumulated complexity was the area below every blog post with a series of features for letting visitors share a post to their social network or rate it on a scale from 1 to 5. Each of these features was created in isolation. They looked and behaved differently; combined, they made blog posts ugly and confusing. I didn't understand how designers could allow something that appeared prominently on every blog post to look so bad. It was the broken window theory gone wrong. I dubbed it NASCAR in reference to how race cars are covered from front to

back with logos from different companies, creating a horror show
of clashing styles.

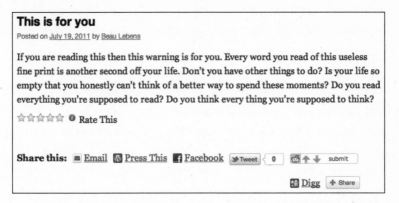

In what would prove to be one the great underestimations of all
time, I asked Beau and Hugo to work on a side project to clean up
NASCAR. The design and technical challenges seemed simple, but
we were all surprised at how hard the engineering of WordPress made
this problem to solve. WordPress excelled at allowing programmers
to add new features. If all we wanted to do was add yet another wid-
get to NASCAR, it'd have been easy. But to make all these features
work together required rewriting them. Each one had been built differently, with little thought for the existence of others. There were
easy rewards for launching new features in the WordPress community, but it was much harder work to consolidate and simplify, so few
did. It took weeks of frustrating work and required great persistence
on Beau's, Hugo's, and my part to get it done, but we did eventually ship an improved version. But the project ran against the flow
of work at the company, and some questioned if it was worth the
trouble. I'm convinced it was. If we couldn't show polish for one of
the few things we make every visitor to WordPress.com see, we had
no right to claim that we cared about quality design at all.

In any organization, large projects require leverage, but few
employees have any. People who have grand ideas but little influence wonder why no one supports them. They think the lack of

support is a judgment on their ideas rather than the politics of authority. Ideas are evaluated differently depending on the mouth they come out of. At Automattic, authority rested in the hands of Matt, Toni, some of the team leads, and a few of the most respected programmers. But even among them, there were rarely big campaigns for new ideas or rethinking big assumptions. The short attention spans born from working online meant that P2 posts with grand ideas, ones that demanded deep thinking for the reader, were overlooked in favor of ones that were easy to respond to (a common occurrence in online discussions known as the bikeshed problem, or Parkinson's law of triviality).[2]

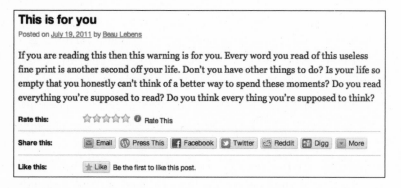

For whatever reason, attention spans or something else, the culture was conservative. Most work stayed on familiar turf and stuck to incremental thinking.[3] It's true that WordPress.com was always improving and there was no crisis to motivate a culture shift. But at the same time, problems that required deeper thinking and bigger bets rarely improved. Even when a debate surfaced about a larger issue, few knew how to convert that debate into a plan.

But every now and then, someone grabbed a big idea and ran with it, clouding my criticisms about Automattic culture. I participated in one of these curveball situations at the Team NUX (New User Experience) meet-up in San Diego in April 2011. While my team plugged along on Jetpack through that spring, I sought other teams to influence. I convinced Nikolay Bachiyski, team lead for NUX, to take on an idea called Writing Helpers. The concept was to build features aimed at helping bloggers make their way through the hurdles of finding ideas and writing drafts. One feature allowed copies of existing posts to be made (Copy A Post), a simple kind of templating. Another feature, Request Feedback, allowed bloggers to e-mail a draft of an unpublished post to friends. My goal was to get them to invest in these ideas and collaborate with Team Social on more in the future.

One afternoon after lunch, designer Noël Jackson and I ranted about things on WordPress.com we thought could be better. The WordPress.com home page was discussed, and we agreed it had major problems. It was odd that the Sign Up button, the most important button on the page, was on the right side of the screen. It's basic design knowledge that people who use Western languages read left to right, meaning that what you put on the left is seen first. We rallied on the many reasons that it was worth trying the other way and about how odd it was that we hadn't tried it. The company had done many A/B tests and redesigns, but somehow this critical real estate had been ignored. Just as there was no team for the store, there was no team for the home page either.

Finally Noël shook his head and went to grab his laptop. I asked him what he was doing, and he said, "I'm fixing this now." And he did. In a few minutes, he rewrote the code for the page to move the bar to the left. We'd also discussed simplifying the design, which he did. Evan Solomon, an expert with A/B testing, helped us measure the impact. This simple change improved signups by 10 percent. Ten minutes of work for a 10 percent increase in one of our primary metrics: an amazing payoff for the price of low-hanging fruit.

This story exemplifies my confusion over Automattic, and it reflects what Lance Willet had said to me back at Seaside: "Welcome to the Chaos." Big opportunities were everywhere, but few grabbed them. Was it a risk-averse culture, despite how much freedom there was to take risks? Was it the personalities of the people hired? Was it a side effect of team divisions? Was it something about P2s? Or was it an effect of the behavior Matt and

Toni cultivated? In fact, all of these were factors. It took only ten minutes of work by Noel to remind me both how open the playing field was at Automattic and at the same time how few were willing to grab the ball and run with it. It was a cultural paradox I still have not resolved.

When Mullenweg hired me, I promised periodic e-mails with observations about the company. As an author, I often visit companies to speak but also spend time with project teams, reporting to executives on what I observe. In February 2011, I sent a long summary to Mullenweg capturing my thoughts. Many of these observations were things I'd posted about on P2s (e.g., "The Limits of P2s") and discussed with Team Social or other Automatticians, but it was the first time I consolidated my observations into a singular list:

Things I've noticed:

1. *Broken windows: good and bad.* It's deep in the culture that things should be fixed immediately. This is great. People take pride in keeping things working. But there is definite ADD—people tend to respond to the most recent thing, not the most important thing. Developers definitely stay busy, but I don't think we're good, as a culture, at ensuring the most important work gets done. We should have a real issue priority system (pri 1 = wp.com down, pri 2 = data loss, etc.) since without it, all issue reporting is very subjective, and we default to "fix it now." It doesn't need to be—it'd make prioritizing for devs/teams easier.

2. *Big/Ugly projects we avoid.* I've noticed that one of the worst usability issues for wp.org is Media—inserting a picture is still a painful. Why hasn't it been fixed? In part, because it's a messy coding/architecture problem (so I've heard) and no one really wants to

take it on. We have similar stories in Automattic (the Store has a similar rep for being a bear to work on). And important things can be broken for weeks or months when they fall off the radar (e.g. LinkedIn Plugin). I'm all for incrementalism but some projects are harder to take on this way. I bet every team has a pile of important things they've basically mothballed that we pretend isn't on the floor. [WordPress 3.5, released in December 2012, redesigned this feature.]

3. *P2s have curious side effects.* Generally I like P2s. But I'm fascinated by which posts generate responses and which are ignored. There's randomness to it (perhaps generated by the volume of p2 activity). It's hard to know when posting on a particular P2 who has read it and who hasn't, and whether a lack of response = implicit approval. I think some people are afraid to post on P2s since they think it's a megaphone and everyone is reading (including you / Toni / etc.). Not sure what I'd change—I think leads & teams need to actively balance out these problems with communication in non-broadcast channels, including meet-ups.

4. *Conservative ideas.* I don't see many people push for big changes, big ideas or crazy thoughts—we're very tactical idea wise—many inspirations are drawn from what competitors are doing. This is ok—we're doing well—but there's not a lot of high powered, crazy ideas kicked around. Not sure why (perhaps #3 above). You seem open to big ideas, but I see it so rarely on P2s. The last big idea I saw was Lenny's post [David Lenehan] on the PollDaddy P2 about going entirely free. My only one so far was on the Writing Helpers (which I think is hugely important) and even that's tame. We have a cultural of tactical thinkers.

Leads should be doing more—and also encouraging their teams. Jetpack is a big idea, but it was yours:)

5. *Talent, camaraderie and morale are high.* I've told you before but this is the secret sauce that makes everything about Automattic work. I can't emphasize enough how critical this is—you've done very well in this regard. Most of the symptoms expressed in this list are compensated for by this fact.

6. *Some things are opaque.* Transparency is very high but there are things no one seems to know. 1) How people are compensated 2) How people are hired (criteria for picking people for trial offers / full time offers). #1 is tricky, but #2 isn't. Leads, at minimum, should know more about the process and be involved you should be teaching us how you've done #5 so well.

7. *Lack of usability methods.* I don't think wordpress.com is as easy to use as we think it is. There are some quick and dirty techniques for evaluating UI, existing code as well as in mockups. I've yet to see anyone propose them or talk about them. Example: I think our dashboard is pretty hard to navigate—it's huge and confusing now. But we have no way of discovering this is a problem (it won't appear as a ticket really), or identifying where the major pain points are. There are ways to do it and we should start. After Jetpack I can take some leadership here.

I'd been trying on my own team to address the first two with the ambitious projects we chose. I'd written about the limits of P2s on a P2, an irony that wasn't lost on me. But many of the rest were deep in the culture and hard to change. Founder-centric companies, which most start-ups are, are a double-edged sword. The initial big ideas come from one person, which, if they are good, is fantastic for early growth. But as the company matures, the need for more people with similar courage increases. If Toni and Matt wanted more people to take risks, they needed to hire and coach for it, which worked against the hands-off, autonomous culture they'd created. There was one team making big bets on what was called The Reader, a radically simplified user experience for blogging. But that project was led by Mullenweg and his Janitorial team, which rarely did janitorial work anymore (he'd later let another Automattician lead the project and give the team a proper name).

Mullenweg acknowledged my e-mail, but we never went through it together, as he'd heard much of it before in Skype or on P2s. My primary responsibility was Team Social, which was doing well, and I didn't see reason to push my feedback further. My work with NUX and other teams gave me plenty of influence to try and earn. If nothing else, I felt my raising these issues planted seeds if someone raised them again.

By May 2011 Team Social had spent six months focused on Jetpack and was known as *the* Jetpack team. This was a problem. The goal was to make Jetpack simply another way for anyone to release features. If Team Social kept driving Jetpack releases, other teams wouldn't learn to do it themselves. I told Mullenweg we'd return to Highlander and other projects. Our next team meet-up was scheduled for Portland, Oregon, a great time to shift the direction of the team.

A good sign as a leader is when output is high and meetings are short. This means all pistons are firing, there are few roadblocks, and things are on track with just a soft touch. It also means meetings can be used to stay ahead, flagging issues before they become blockers. Managers often wrap their egos around meetings, and long meetings ensure they always feel that they're the center of attention, even if the meeting is a waste of time for everyone else. I was proud to see, at one meeting before Portland, that most of the conversation was simply about Beau's new knife and its implications for team safety:

mdawaffe: berkun Sorry you had to resort to Skype, didn't see your note here

berkun: no worries

berkun: I thought it was funny to put out a cry for help and have no one respond. What if I was drowning?

mdawaffe: then you should be asking for help from those near you

berkun: they should list as a downside to distributed teams: 'can't help when you're drowning'

mdawaffe: upside: less likely to be brutally murdered by axe wielding psychopath coworker

mdawaffe: what do you think the A is in apeatling?

mdawaffe: "Axe-Wileding"

berkun: hmm. Maybe I should get sick this weekend and not go to Portland. Might up odds of surviving to June

berkun: if Peatling has an Axe and Beau has a new knife (to add to his *collection*), you and I need to get armed.

mdawaffe: hm—good point

berkun: Does sarcasm count as a weapon?

mdawaffe: lets just push Hugo towards them and run

berkun: ah. Nice.

Unable to find an apartment like we had in New York City, I discovered an Embassy Suites hotel in Portland with one room with a large work space and conference table, suitable as our headquarters for the week. Andrew Spittle, one of the happiness engineers who trained me when I was hired, and Alex Mills, a programmer on the VIP team, lived in Portland, and they joined us for much of the meet-up.

The goal was simple: finish phase 1 of Highlander, which meant launching our new user interface for commenting on WordPress.com blogs. We hadn't touched the project since Athens, forcing us to pay the tax of refilling our brains with everything we'd forgotten. But in just two days, we had the balance of the functionality working well, leaving us three days to finish. Much like our New York City meet-up, our time in Portland was mostly spent working long hours. We fell into a routine of meeting for breakfast, joining at the conference table for a half-day of work, a short break for lunch, and another long session before a late dinner. Often we'd work again after dinner and late into the night. Portland was a comfortable city, easy to walk around, with many pubs, cafés, and a legendary set of food carts for lunch. Beau, always in search of the highest-calorie meal on earth, discovered the Redonkadonk, a massive caloric bomb inspired by a cheeseburger but with two grilled cheese sandwiches for buns, and Spam, bacon, and American cheese to supplement an oversized beef patty. We also snuck away for an afternoon of retrogaming on classic arcade games and beers at Ground Kontrol.

All of our meet-ups were highlighted by the discovery of a comfortable place to spend long hours, a place that was our second home. We were lucky to find those places: they were key parts of why the meet-ups worked well. In Athens it was the quiet balcony bar with Mythos and spicy potato chips. In New York, it was our comfortable SoHo apartment, a venue we'd never replicate. In Portland it would turn out to be an out-of-the-way sports bar, the Life of Riley Tavern. Each night we took over the back of the dimly lit bar for its mini-shuffleboard table, and we'd talk, drink, and play until it was time to go home. It was at this bar that Hugo, who had been one of the quieter members of the team, finally felt comfortable joining our sarcastic mockery of each other. Games let everyone take on a different role, dropping whatever pretense for status there is among coworkers. At a big corporation, an evening at Life of Riley's would be called a morale event, but I hate that term. Morale isn't an event; it's the accumulated goodwill people build through work together. Our time at Life of Riley gave us a new way to relate to each other and know each other better, something games do magically well. We rarely talked about work or Automattic out at Life of Riley's. We'd return home late at night with new stories about each other to share, and new running jokes and references that always ended up in our work interactions, spicing them up and keeping us laughing and engaged.

These evenings centered on the deceptively simple game of shuffleboard. You slide a puck across the board and hope it stops in a marked area, worth 1, 2, or 4 points. But the board is covered with sand, making every slight adjustment in velocity and angle amplified: most shots fly right off the edge. If you do land a puck for points, the other team, on its turn, can knock your puck off the board. As we improved, we figured out how to use pucks to protect other pucks, creating the basics of offensive and defensive strategies. We played two on two, with the fifth person acting as referee (indicating how serious these games became). While the games started out fun, they became intense. Peatling showed his British roots, an innate mastery of all pub games, including, to our surprise, shuffleboard. I lost dozens of close and not-so-close games to him, but I'd have a reckoning with him on the board before the trip was over.

The Highlander project moved along well; each hour of each day saw us knock more items off our lists. But as we approached the final push, we sensed we'd overlooked something. Something important. Back in Athens, we had run into the project trap of postponing little things no one wanted to do to the end, when they cost more to do. But in Portland, despite starting from where we'd left off in Athens and working hard for days, we ran into the same trap again. We discovered the project trap is recursive: even when working within a list of postponed things, you still postpone things no one wants to do. And this time it was a special project twilight zone trap, the kind that occurs when cathedral ideas collided with bazaar practices:

- Cathedral ideal: Unify and simplify the experience of comments across all WordPress.com blogs.
- Bazaar reality: There were 120 blog themes, each with a unique comments design.

Similar to NASCAR, each theme was built independently, without anyone imagining someone might want to unify how commenting worked. What had been an advantage at the time— creating many different-looking themes to let users personalize their websites—was now a liability in the goal to unify them. Ever the compromiser, I asked Matt if he was okay if we launched Highlander on the top ten or twenty themes and supported more over time, but he pushed us to go for it all in one shot. We dug into the details, and it was demoralizing. We talked over several different approaches, but for testing Highlander with different web designs, which was effectively what each theme was, and across different browsers, there was no fast way. We'd need to look at them all by hand and report bugs.

But in what was a triumph of Automattic culture, the cavalry arrived. We asked the Theme Team for help, and they converted dozens of themes to use a common piece of code, simplifying our work. Then from our conference table in Portland, we posted on our P2 and others asking the entire company to help test specific themes and report bugs. Fourteen people joined in, including Andrew and Alex, in one of the longest P2 threads I'd seen—over sixty posts, each helping us on our way. It was a virtual barn raising—the community dropping their own work to help us finish something important. It was Team Social and Automattic working at its best. It was a combination of programmers, designers, and happiness engineers, some local, some remote, all working together to deliver on a single grand idea.

Even with all the help, the work was grueling. With two days to go, I had to make sure we paced ourselves. It was another unspoken leader task: finding the sweet spot of breaks and meals to keep people productive without burning them out. One night I did the team lead chore of warning everyone we'd leave for dinner in ten minutes. I'd learned that if I didn't make these warnings loud and enforce them by closing people's laptops, we'd work until someone was burned out, irritable, and starving, spoiling morale for the day. That night, when Peatling heard the announcement, he yelled out, "It's the final countdown!" and began humming the melody to the ridiculous 1980s power ballad by the band Europe. Beau found the song on YouTube and blasted it on his speakers. A perfect way to end a long day.[4]

On our last night, with the project mostly finished, we made our way back to Riley's for one last series of games. Beau and I were finally ahead in a close match against Adams and Peatling. For days we'd all wanted to beat Peatling, and we were all excited that now we had our chance. The score stayed close, with us always ahead but not by much. On our team's last throw, I pinned our final blue puck in a perfect position, protecting our winning score. It was a fantastic throw, bumping a puck into the four-points area, and shielding it at the same time. Beau and I went wild. The game was basically over. Peatling had a last throw, but there was no way to get around my shield puck and the other pucks on the board.

Peatling sized up the table, and Adams, his teammate, looked at the different angles, offering the pretense of advice. As was our way, Beau and I dished out the best trash talk we could, high-fiving each other in what seemed to be an impossible-to-lose situation. Provided the laws of physics didn't change in the next minute, the only way they could win was if Peatling sent a miracle curveball around my last throw, past one of his own red pucks that was also blocking the shot, and then somehow, using the force, bent it back at a thirty-degree angle in the opposite direction to knock our team's puck off the board. In all of our play all week, we'd never seen anyone make a shot half as difficult.

He measured and measured again, shaking off the effect of a good night's drinking. He was all business, not answering any of our taunts or Adams's advice. With his glare fixed on the table, he measured the angles and spins in his mind. And then with one final motion, he flicked his arm across the table and let it go. He spun the puck hard, betting he could make it bend across the board like a curveball, creating just enough room for a workable angle. I watched it move, thinking for sure he'd thrown it too hard and confident it would go off the edge like so many other throws we'd seen. But it didn't. Just when it should have stayed straight or been too strong and missed its mark, it did the inconceivable; Peatling's spin, taking full effect, slid the puck past his others and directly into mine. My puck flew, in embarrassed disgrace, to the side, and his replaced it for a four-point score. The game was over. Again we'd lost.

It was the most amazing thing I'd seen in a pub game, so fantastic that instead of wallowing, Beau and I, just like everyone else, were yelling and screaming at this amazing throw. The rest of Life of Riley's looked on at a bunch of crazy kids, dancing around at a silly game. But to us it was something else, a story we'd share dozens of times in the months to come.

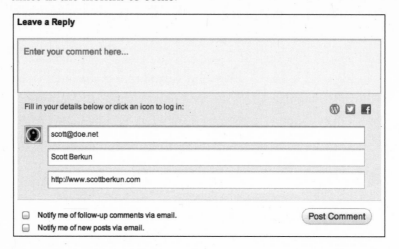

We launched Highlander inside Automattic on May 25 to give us more time to fully test all of the themes. Even after the meet-up, we continued to find small issues, which we prioritized and fixed in the week that followed. On June 7 we launched the first part of Highlander to the world and put in place a framework that made the future of comments much stronger for WordPress. We did various A/B test experiments, looking for ways to simplify the design, but we learned that the most important factor in encouraging comments was the blogger's post. There was only so much the user interface itself could do. But even on the first day, 300,000 new comments were published through Highlander, and more every day since.

CHAPTER 22

THE BUREAU OF SOCIALIZATION

Over the summer and fall of 2011, Team Social changed dramatically. While we continued to chase our goals, improving Highlander and making posting easier, our roster was shaken up. Peatling left our group in a trade with the Janitorial team. We acquired Justin Shreve, one of the youngest programmers in the company, still in college for his bachelor's degree. Matt and I had talked about the swap weeks earlier, and I agreed these moves were great. The best way to share knowledge is to share people. As sad as it was for a closely knit team like ours to lose someone, everybody wins in the long term. Our team also doubled in size, adding programmers John Jacoby and Tim Moore. John, living in Wisconsin, was a WordPress veteran but new to WordPress.com. Tim, from Maine, had been a jack of all trades for a university, and Automattic was by far the biggest company he'd worked at. Team Social would be his first time working on a team of programmers. I was happy to see the team grow. Our goals had always been ambitious, and now we had more resources to work with to deliver.

By the fall it was time for our next meet-up, and we chose Lisbon, Portugal, for a good reason: Hugo Baeta, our designer, lived there. We timed our visit to coincide with WordCamp Lisbon, which he helped organize, and it was the first official WordPress event in the country. This was a common planning trick for meet-ups. It let us contribute something to the WordPress community by participating in the event but also let us escape to do new work. Isaac Keyet and Jorge Bernal from the Mobile team joined, flying in from Denmark and Spain, respectively. We rented what we thought was a big apartment that, to our disappointment, had very low, angular ceilings. This led to our first bet of the trip: Who would be the first teammate to bang his head? Many would suffer memorable wounds and spend the trip with hunched shoulders in an attempt to avoid further injury. Moore couldn't make the trip to Lisbon so we Skyped him in for meetings out on the sunny patio of our Lisbon apartment. Peatling came along as a last mission with his former teammates (and I made sure there were no shuffleboard tables within five kilometers of him or our team).

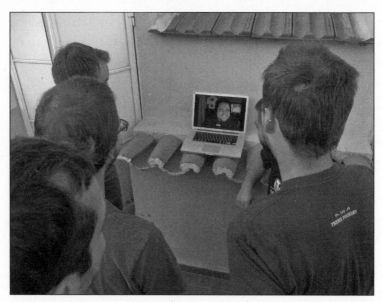

At night, to take breaks from work, we wandered out on Lisbon's beautiful black and white stone streets to small shops near parks and major streets, that served beer and snacks outside. It was a beautiful, if run-down, city, the proud sailing symbols of its seafaring culture everywhere we looked. While it was hard to find pubs open as late as we'd found in Athens, the kiosks became our second home. And instead of our masochistic ouzo rituals Hugo took us out for ginjinha, a bittersweet liquor made from cherries, at the oldest hole-in-the-wall tavern in town that served it, called, predictably, Café A Ginjinha.

The growth of our team meant important changes for me. The slice of attention I had for each person was smaller. Seven people is on the edge of wanting to be two mini-teams, one of three and one of four. And the new folks, John and Tim, naturally needed help to get up to speed. The wisest solution to my challenges was to create room for new leaders to step up. For this I looked to Adams and Beau. For months before Lisbon, I'd chatted with them often on Skype about issues larger than their work assignments. They helped me manage trial projects for hiring candidates and gave opinions on tough decisions. I depended on them, and with Peatling's departure, it was easy to see them as my senior staff.

The transition to managing a larger team reminded me that when everything is going fine, management is easy. Thousands of managers around the world inherit healthy teams in healthy companies, do little of merit, and get great rewards for just being in the right place at the right time. The real story behind some people you meet with fantastic reputations isn't notable talents or skills, but merely an exceptional ability to choose the right time to join and leave particular projects. The work of managers everywhere is rarely evaluated with enough consideration for the situation they inherited and the situations they faced that were not in their control. We all make judgments of ability at the most superficial levels. If the results are good, we give praise. If the results are poor, we criticize. We rarely give credence to the feeling in the back of our minds that the winner or loser doesn't quite fit the part. We know in our careers people who were shafted, taking the fall for incompetence that wasn't theirs, and also people who slide through organizations as if coated with Teflon, causing misery and frustration at every turn, yet they move into promotions unscathed.

This isn't so much a complaint as an observation. Looking solely at the results of an organization from the outside tells you little about its leaders. The charge of an executive, a basketball coach, or even a president of a nation requires study to evaluate. Perhaps these people had a fantastic supporting cast that buffered the rest of the organization from their incompetence. Or their brilliance was shattered to pieces by scandals, conspiracies, and disasters driven by coworkers hired before they arrived, challenges no one could endure. Among the clues for sorting out the truth is how a leader handles things going wrong—not the show that happens in front of crowds but in the daily meetings and decisions where there is no audience. If they genuinely share credit but take the lion's share of blame, you might just have someone sincerely invested in doing what's best. A leader who shields others from things that get in the way inspires everyone to do the same. It's small habits like these that shift a culture away from the pointless exercises of finger pointing and dodging blame and toward a contagious confidence that the best work of your career is possible *right now*. The feeling that there's nothing in your way is something few feel often in their careers, if they ever feel it at all.

What made work at Automattic fun and challenging was how often things changed. You never knew what the week was going to throw at you. While our goals, our support from Matt and Toni, and the basic mechanics of P2s, Skype, and continuous deployment were steady, many things were in constant motion. Working on a live service meant daily, sometimes hourly, shifts of resources to fix urgent bugs or help another team in a bind. Often Adams and Beau were called in as experts to help the Happiness team fix a difficult problem or meet with VIP clients to teach. This was part of the way Automattic worked, and you had to roll with it. What you put in, you generally got back, if not more, as Team Social often benefited from help from the NUX, Data, Theme, and Happiness teams.

The team meet-ups were always special for me not simply because we had fun and were productive, but in that they were special opportunities for experiments. It's easier to get feedback and make adjustments with how a team works if you're in the same room. Feedback is hard to come by in life at all. It's easy to give the pretense of feedback: anyone can say to a coworker, "Do you have any feedback for me?" and for the person to say, "No. Not really," and then for you to say, "Okay, great. Thanks!" and walk off having validated all of your bogus assumptions about your awesomeness for another year. The reality check is to consider how many things you've wanted to say to people you've worked with that if they were open to it, could have helped them do better work but that you've been afraid to mention.

Automattic was a hard place to get feedback. You had to go out of your way on Skype and reach for it, and as a lead, I knew it was my job to be a primary source of feedback for the people on my team. By Lisbon, I'd experimented enough to build three traditions into our meet-ups to ensure channels of frequent high-quality feedback:

1. *First-night dinner.* I always asked everyone to arrive by the afternoon on the first day. This guaranteed we'd meet for a big dinner on the first night to kick off the week. We'd catch up on everything in each other's personal lives and reconnect without an agenda.
2. *Projects decided at first night.* The one mandatory topic at first night was deciding what project to work on. This decision was something of a ruse since I always knew well before we arrived what the project was going to be. I used the suspense to draw people out and hear what they were excited about. I also wanted to see them pitch each other and me on why they thought one thing was more valuable than another.
3. *One-on-ones.* During the meet-up, I'd schedule time with everyone to talk in private. The conversation centered on the same four big personal questions I asked everyone in e-mail once a month: What's going well? What's not? What do you want me to do more of? What do you want me to do less of?

Specific to Mike and Beau, I had another kind of experiment in mind. Could I help them grow into future leads for Automattic? First, it would help me and Team Social in the short term. But second, and more important for Automattic, I could let them start to see things from the leader's view. Things look different from the captain's chair, and I wanted them to get comfortable. When working distributedly, I'd often end meetings with the entire team and immediately grab Mike or Beau, or both, and have a different kind of chat about the week ahead. I needed them to help show the folks the ropes. I had Beau work with John and Mike with Tim. Justin surprised us all by fitting right in without a hitch, and soon he was setting the pace as the most productive programmer on the team.

Tim and Hugo both had a hard time acclimating to Automattic. They both saw the constant stream of activity running by on our and other P2s and had trouble figuring out how to step in. There was pressure for both of them to fit into their dream job, as they'd been fans of WordPress for many years. And with the awareness that P2s are visible to everyone, a certain psychological trap exists for new hires. It's easy to get stuck in a place where you're not contributing much but are too scared to take big bets in such a new place. It was my job to pick up where their tour in Happiness left off. I could do more to help Hugo since I was a designer, but the playbook was the same for both:

1. Break assignments into smaller pieces
2. If there is no progress, go to #1 and repeat.

WordPress programmers generally shot from the hip because web development rewards quick prototyping. But Tim and Hugo were more methodical. Tim needed to dig in deep to a code base before he'd be comfortable making changes. I worked with him over his first weeks to narrow assignments and find bugs in working code at the sweet spot between his comfort level and work we needed done. I had Adams mentor him, answering coding questions I couldn't but also providing an example to emulate for Automattic attitudes about programming. It was slow at first, but Tim took to Jetpack, and he soon became the primary person for handling the continual bug fixing and tweaking it demanded. With the steady support he got from the rest of the team, his confidence and productivity rose.

For Hugo the big discovery was comfort showing what he considered unfinished work. It's a common weakness among creatives, whether a designer, a writer, or a programmer, to be shy about showing unfinished work. Creators love control over their pixels and bits and to share work before it's done is to give up all sense of control. But the value of having a designer on any project at any company is involving them early. They can try out ideas in sketches faster and cheaper than any other profession can. As a writer, I know exactly how limiting words can be to express ideas, and until Hugo's hiring, it was up to me to constantly sketch and mock up ideas others were discussing on our P2.

Once Hugo realized how helpful it was to post hand-drawn sketches and ideas, even if he was sketching ideas from other people, he soared. It told him it didn't matter if the sketches were "right"; what mattered was that his sketch improved the quality of the conversation, which it always did. He partnered well with Beau on NASCAR and other projects, earning our trust as someone, as Joen did early on Jetpack, who could drive vague ideas to clarity. And beyond everything else, he made our work look great. After taking us to A Tapadinha, a fantastic Russian-themed restaurant in Lisbon he found in honor of our team name, he redesigned our theme borrowing some of its Soviet aesthetic.

While in Lisbon, another experiment we tried was using tools other than our trusted P2/Skype IRC combo. We'd all heard about many new tools that claimed to help collaboration or work flow, and I wanted to see if they would help us. The results, after hours of trying, were clear: it was a disaster. Between connectivity issues, lag, compatibility, and usability problems, we spent more time trying to get these tools to work reliably than actually doing our project work with them. I'm sure these tools had a learning curve, but the reliability and speed of P2 and Skype trumped everything we tried. For all of the interesting features, like virtual whiteboards and seven-way videoconferencing, they came at the expense of annoyances and lags that made them more trouble than they were worth. The sad testament to our experimental results was that after nearly two hours, we had one screen of doodles on a whiteboard to show for our efforts. The experiment may have gone better in the sanctity of a corporate wi-fi network, but with my team on the road around the world, these tools wouldn't survive.

Two months after Lisbon, Team Social would meet again for the big company meeting in Budapest. The company had grown to over one hundred people, twice the size of when I was hired. Budapest was chosen since one-third of the employees were based in Europe and all previous meetings had been in North America.

Unlike the company meeting in Seaside, there were major curveballs this time:

1. Everyone worked on new teams formed just for the meet-up.
2. Projects were picked by Mullenweg based on suggestions.
3. Every team would have a new lead, someone who'd never led before.
4. Each team had to present to the company on the last day.
5. The goal was to ship something before the presentation.

It was brilliant. The Seaside meet-up had gone well, but this one raised the stakes. I loved everything about it. Even better, Mullenweg gave me a gift: I was assigned to a pet project of mine. If you recall, I wanted to improve what happened when a user managed to publish a new blog post.

Here, for the last time in this book, is my theory of blogging:

**Get idea → Draft Post → Edit Post → Publish →
Hope something happens**

After all the hurdles, WordPress gave no payoff that you'd done well. There should be fireworks, praise, dancing kittens—anything that made you look forward to the next time you'd be at this screen again. Over the months I'd worked with Peatling to make improvements, and Team Janitorial developed it further, but it still had a long way to go.

In Budapest I was assigned to the Post Postmodernism team, which had the goal of improving the post post, or the thing you see after you post something. The team was led by Mo Jangda (VIP team, based in Toronto), Daryl Koopersmith (.org team, San Francisco), Matías Ventura (Theme team, based in Uruguay), Shaun Andrews (VaultPress team, New York), and Ran Harstein (Happiness team, Israel). We met on day 1 and got to work.

The first day of a new team on a short deadline is fascinating anthropology. Everyone tries to figure everyone else out—who is talented, who has the same taste, who is easy or hard to work with, who has status—all at the same time they're trying to figure out the project itself. And at Automattic there's the wrinkle of everyone relearning how to work in the same physical place, where verbal persuasion returns to the mix of influences. I was immediately impressed with Daryl and Matías, who liked to work hard and welcomed input on everything they did. Mo helped set the pace, making sure everyone had a task and was moving forward. In a hodgepodge, chaotic way, we slowly progressed as new ideas came up and prototypes were offered; rough consensus was the way of the day.

The big decision we had to make was what user interface model to use. We had several ideas, and I sketched them out, following my own advice to Hugo to make things visible. The original design was B, with a small section appearing above the edit screen. But Mo and others thought we should double down and go with design C, entirely replacing the edit screen with the user's actual post. There was good support for this: the data we had suggested that 25 percent of users viewed their post right away. We bet this was to check for typos and to bask in the glory of their finally finished work. Daryl pointed out we could make this pivotal decision late in the game. The hard work would be deciding what the gray box should do. What should the payoff be? How do we reward users for their work?

Each day was a sprint, jumping back and forth between meeting together, working on our P2, and chatting on Skype. Slowly the focus shifted from mock-ups by Matías, Shaun, and me, to coding by Mo and Daryl. We added a sharing section, based on data we had about people's habits for wanting to share their work on Facebook and Twitter, and if they had Publicize turned on, we'd show the results of how many people in their social network their new post had been automatically shared to.

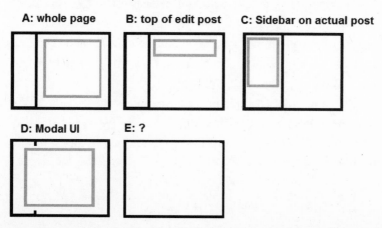

It was a whirlwind of work, with Mo, Matías, and Daryl doing more than the rest of us. I mocked up screens, fought for ideas, and found lots of bugs, but it was those three who made hope of launching by meet-up's end possible. Mo asked me to do the presentation to the company, and as I put it together, it wasn't clear if we'd be able to launch in time. Minutes before I stood up to speak, Mo managed to get everything launched: our creation was live to the world. As I walked through the demonstration, I proudly explained our work had been launched live to 10 percent of all WordPress.com users, with trackers in place so we could observe how this sample responded to all the changes we made.

In six days, five people who had never worked together before planned, designed, and launched a feature millions of people would use. For all my planning, scheming, and influencing as a team lead, sometimes talent, chaos, and chemistry are all you need for good work. What's hardest of all to believe is that every one of the twelve teams shipped their projects to the world that day. We'd never be able to repeat sprints like this every week, but the thrill of trying so many experiments at once energized us all for months to come.

CHAPTER 23

EXIT THROUGH HAWAII

My last meet-up with Team Social was in Hawaii in January 2012. I can't remember how we decided on Hawaii. Whatever rationalization we told ourselves was far from the truth. We simply all wanted to go to Hawaii. Other teams had been there, and most of our team was on the West Coast with Hugo's recent move to San Francisco. The story we told Matt, but more so to ourselves, was to switch priorities for locations each meet-up: we'd alternate between exotic (Athens, Lisbon, and now Hawaii) and practical (Portland, New York City). Hawaii, assuming we could rent a house for cheap lodging and cook many of our own meals, wasn't more expensive than any other trip for seven people located across the country. We rented a house with a fantastic view out the kitchen window of what were called the friendship trees. We'd see locals meet here with friends to go surfing while we made dinner for ourselves.

The challenge for this meet-up was that I'd known for months that it was time for me to leave. I'd planned to work for Automattic for a year, but that date had come and gone long ago. Mullenweg had asked me periodically to take on more responsibility and manage other teams beyond Team Social, and I'd turned him down. As tempting as it was each time, these conversations reminded me I needed an exit strategy.

Of the many dreams I've had in my life, making great software is one. But the biggest, craziest, and most rewarding dream to chase has been the writing life. If what I wanted most from my time at work was to make software, I'd have stayed. But that wasn't my biggest dream. I'd already stayed longer than I'd planned. We all imagine an angel will fly down from the sky and let us know it's time to make that change we've had on our minds for far too long. But that angel never comes because that angel doesn't exist. It's a fantasy born of our lack of faith in our own ideas. For me, leaving would mean I could start working on a book about my time at Automattic, a contribution I believed would be more important than my involvement with any number of teams.

The last act of good leaders is to ensure things go well when they're gone. Many legendary leaders failed at this: Alexander the Great, Julius Caesar, Napoleon, and nearly every monarch in history. As much good as they did in their reigns, most of it was undone by those who followed. The same ego that drives grand leaders defeats them in the end because they can't accept the notion that someone will replace them. Succession planning must be part of any long-term leader's thinking, and it has to be done now. Not all exits from leadership roles are voluntary, either due to the Brutus in your midst or the bus you forget to notice when crossing a street you've crossed a thousand times before.

I told Mullenweg late in 2011, around the time of Budapest, that I would be making my exit soon. We had long Skype chats about who should replace me as lead and had two candidates: Adams and Beau. Thinking selfishly, I'd have been happy to work for either of them. Both had the right diversity of skills, attitudes, and interests to do much more than programming. We decided on Adams in part for his tenure at the company, but it'd be splitting hairs to dissect it even that far. With Matt's agreement on the decision, the next moves were mine. It wasn't clear Adams wanted the job, and I had to make sure every detail was resolved before anyone on my team got on a plane to meet in Hawaii.

To offer Adams the job meant disclosing my leaving, and once that ice is broken, it's best to let everyone know quickly. No one should be expected to carry the burden of a secret their peers would love to know. I talked it over with Adams and explained the situation and the offer. He thought it over briefly and said yes. Next up was to talk to Beau. He deserved to be the first to know and to hear it directly from me. We talked over Skype voice, and I did my best to explain everything. I'd recommended to Matt that Beau become a lead soon and made sure Beau knew that. I asked him to be discrete and grant his teammates the same courtesy I'd granted him of hearing the news from me. I encouraged Adams to ping Beau and for them to talk to get any awkwardness quickly out of the way. They've been good friends for longer than Team Social existed, and the sooner they started talking about the future, the better.

The first night, after everyone arrived at our beach house, I pulled people aside by the pool one by one to break the news. Some were surprised; others, like Hugo, had known me long enough to think the writing was on the wall. They took it well, as chaos is expected among Automatticians. When everyone knew, we had a grand meal at our home for the week and toasted Adams as the new czar of the Bureau of Socialization. We all helped to cook enormous, delicious, blatantly unhealthy, carnivorous meals—trays of bacon from the oven, fresh guacamole, and steaks—and drank Margaritas out of paper cups like college students (which Justin still was), and made the house our own. We ate every kind of Oreo we could find, and wished many of them, particularly the ones flavored with Strawberry, had never been invented. On one rare night when we went out for dinner, I convinced the restaurant host to let our team take a picture in their kitchen, the last blank in a blank photo I'd ever get to take. Daniel Bachhuber, a programmer on Team VIP, was in town and joined us.

The next day Mullenweg tuned in to chat with us and answer any questions about the leadership change. To his credit, this is precisely the kind of kickoff any new lead deserves. It verified for everyone that the company was behind the change and empowered Adams to have a good start with all the support he needed.

My plan for the meet-up was one last experiment. What would happen if I taught my team tricks for how to think holistically about WordPress? Not about features but about how all the features fit together? There were dozens of fancy methods for teaching people to think this way, and my plan for the meet-up was to teach some to my own team. For the week, we'd go corporate: I got flip charts, a color printer, and a big LCD monitor, and we worked together on exercises reevaluating how good WordPress was. Even before we started, the psychological scale of my experiment was having an effect. The team was mystified by my purchasing a printer, a monitor, and a flip chart, relics of the past. "What is this for?" they asked. "What is wrong with you?" For the first day, it was the new running joke: Is Scott on (more) crack (than usual)? I kept the answer a secret, not wanting to reveal my experiment until they were in it.

Each morning we did what's called a UX walkthrough, walking through one feature, detailing every action and decision a user had to make. Each time we found something confusing, we'd stop, print it out, and put it up on the wall with a note about the usability

problem we discovered. On some days, we couldn't make it ten
seconds without all of us smacking our foreheads at the obvious
usability issues. Each morning we picked a different feature and
walked through it. At the same time, I used usertesting.com to
schedule a remote usability test of the same feature with a real user.
When we finished our walkthrough, we'd watch videotape of a real
user and compare his or her experience. Then in the afternoon, we
each picked one issue and fixed it, making a list of all of the other
issues we didn't get to on the P2.

We were all dumbfounded by how many little things we didn't
realize users needed to understand to get through some of our basic
tasks. Clearly millions of users did get through, but we were certain
that experience was much harder than it needed to be. It wasn't
even anyone's fault: over time, many of the simplest features had
simply been cluttered by add-ons, each done in isolation, much
like NASCAR had been. The last exercise I had everyone do was
a basic planning game. We pulled the most important feature ideas
from our list on our P2, and discussed which ones best fit our goals.
We put each idea on a sticky note and lined them up in order for
the next year. Anyone could change the order at any time, and
we let this happen all week. Like ants moving a twig, each one of

us nudged the list in one direction, and someone else nudged it in another. At first the order changed every few hours, but eventually it gravitated toward a reasonable plan. Midway through the week, I pulled Adams aside to tell him it was time. If he was ready, we should announce he was in charge. It'd be great for everyone to see me following his lead as my role switched to being just an individual designer on the team. I was a lame duck anyway, and as I'd learned, there's more feedback available in real time and space with people. The sooner Adams gained experience, the better. It was the first time I'd hadn't had a leadership role on a project in longer than I could remember, and it felt good. I'd never seen a leader step down before and stay on the same team, yet another experiment to try.

I can't say enough good things about working by the beach. I'd never seen my team so relaxed and so productive when we needed to be. Our second home in Hawaii wasn't a pub or a bar but the water. We'd take breaks in the morning and the afternoon to swim, and the waves would calm everyone down, washing whatever stress had been on our mind from the work of the day. Although we didn't write much code in Hawaii, our time looking at screens, talking, and debating the future, thinking broadly about WordPress instead of just about features, might have mattered more than any feature we'd ever launched. It might take time, but I hoped I planted some seeds that would bear fruit in the years to come. And even if they thought it was all corporate nonsense, they'd have had to respect my willingness to give something this crazy a try.

At 2:00 a.m. on the last night, we all found ourselves outside on the beach. It was warm and quiet, the only sound the rolling of the waves against the sand. A full moon hovered above, shedding a soft warm light on us as we talked. Knowing we'd all have to get up early to catch our flights and this was the last time we'd have, we didn't want it to end. The long, intense days of working, playing in the ocean, and then working late into the evening were over. I stood in the moonlight, lost in my own realization that the night, the meet-up, my tenure as lead, and my time at Automattic were all coming to a close. There was a moment I'll never forget when we all stood out near the water, playing with trashy sand castles built with the spent paper cups that had held our last drinks together, standing quietly, listening to the waves roll in.

CHAPTER 24

THE FUTURE OF WORK, PART 3

Here in the last chapter of the book, I can't tell you to simply copy what Automattic has done. It'd be foolish to tell you that since every company and person is different. But I can tell you this: they have answered many important questions the working world is afraid even to ask.

The most dangerous tradition we hold about work is that it must be serious and meaningless. We believe that we're paid money to compensate us for work not worthwhile on its own. People who are paid the most are often the most confused, for they know in their hearts how little meaning there is in what they do, for others and for themselves. While money provides status, status doesn't guarantee meaning. They're paid well because of how poorly work compensates their souls. Some people don't have souls, of course, but they're beyond the scope of this book. Among those with souls and high-paying but empty jobs, there's a denial of how what they seek is hard to get in the way they're trying to get it.

Earlier in this book I explained the dangers of data-driven thinking and how the most important things are the hardest to capture in numbers. While we have a universal measure of wealth called money, there is no comparable measurement for meaning. Meaning is personal. There is no singular meaning of life; instead there are multitudes, and they're different for everyone. Emotional words like *meaning*, *passion*, and *soul* are scary to people who believe everything in life hinges on pure rationality. With no universal measure for meaning to compare with the seemingly solid accounting for income, we fall into the data trap. Our larger culture, and our pesky parents, push us toward decisions that seem to score well but are blind to the most important elements of healthy careers and meaningful lives. Of course, you can find work that provides both wealth and meaning, but it takes more effort. Many people believe that throughout history, work has rarely given people meaning, but that's not true. The history of work is rooted in survival. We hunted and gathered in order to live. Little distinction was made between work and the rest of life. Rather than this making life miserable, it likely made it more meaningful. Every action, however hard, had personal significance. Working with your own hands to catch a fish or build a shelter gave deep satisfaction that few high-paying jobs ever will. I personally do not possess either of these skills (to Beau's disappointment), but I recognize the distinction between work that matters to me and work that doesn't, and the difference has defined the choices I've made in my career. What I've sacrificed in income has been compensated for in things money can't buy.

In *The History of Work*, Richard Donkin describes how the ancient traditions of the Australian Yir-Yoront tribe, first discovered in 1903 and previously untouched by modern humans, had no distinction between work and play:

> They do have a word—"woq"—that is used to refer to various tasks and chores. But the chores—this woq—did not include hunting. Hunting, the most fundamental activity in a hunter-gathering society, was not viewed as work. Work in this society seemed to be viewed as something they would rather not be doing. Isn't this concept—something I would rather not be doing—one of the most recognizable definitions of work for most of us?[1]

In this sense, companies like Automattic are returning work to its roots. It's not a new, radical idea for work to have meaning and for workers to have both great freedom and pride in the work itself. Instead those ideas are rooted in the origins of work; we've just lost our way. Through the last two centuries, work has become increasingly abstract, which of course, is, in some ways, progress. Fewer people (at least in the First World) are exposed to dangerous, backbreaking labor. But at the same time, we've lost the beneficial effects work used to have on our psychology. In *Shopcraft as Soulcraft*, a book about recovering the lost values of what we call blue-collar work, Matthew Crawford identifies how often we mock the emptiness of modern workplaces: "The popularity of Dilbert, The Office, and any number of other pop-culture windows on cubicle life attests to the dark absurdism with which many Americans have come to view their white-collar work."[2] It has been only in the past hundred years that work has become this way. In the centuries of civilization prior, many more of us had crafts and skills that gave us pride. It might just be that progressive companies like Automattic are open to the idea that technology can return some of the meaning of work we've lost. Even if the work is based on volume, like answering support tickets on Team Happiness, offering a results-first culture empowers people to find their own solutions for when and where to work, benefiting everyone.

Regarding the assumption that work must be serious, a critique I received on drafts of this book was how much time was spent on Team Social adventures together. Few business books, even ones about famous projects, mention the relationships workers have, lending the pretense that they are robots. It was impossible to tell an honest story about a team without some of what happened outside the formal boundaries of life and work, boundaries Automattic was founded on eliminating. Humor was a primary strength of our team. That's not to say hiring clowns to walk your hallways will help, but the denial of joy as a central element of quality work is a mistake. Humor, storytelling, and songs are social skills we developed thousands of years ago around fires while we did the critical work of staying warm and cooking food to survive. It's a shockingly recent notion that work and play should be mutually exclusive things. We learn about ourselves and each other through play, which helps us work together. Not everyone believes this, of course, but I do.

Because of Automattic's open source routes and vision for democratizing publishing, meaning was easy to find. Few other organizations have roots like these, but all leaders can choose to make decisions for the long term. The most profound things about Automattic center on its long-term view of the organization. Every perk, benefit, or experiment ties back to its commitment to build a company for years and perhaps decades into the future. Having deep values is one way to inspire long-term thinking, and any good leader can find others. But long-term commitments demand short-term sacrifices. The question is, How willing are we to make the trade?

EPILOGUE: WHERE ARE
THEY NOW?

- *At Budapest in 2011, I gave a presentation on how I led Team Social.* Mullenweg asked me to give the opening talk at the company meeting, outlining how I defined my role and how the team functioned. A write-up of that talk was made part of the *Company Field Guide* (the employee handbook). Some of the ideas from that talk are in this book.
- *I left Automattic in May 2012.* After stepping down as lead in January, I stayed on with Team Social as a designer and took pleasure at being purely an individual contributor on a team for the first time in seventeen years. When Hugo and I were ahead of the team, I put my energy elsewhere, trying to persuade teams on the need for better user experience thinking and ran some of the first usability studies on WordPress.com. When I left the company, I returned to my writing career to work on my fifth book, the one you're almost finished reading right now.
- *The Highlander project was a moderate success.* It did achieve some of our unification goals but never resulted in the waves of comments we hoped. Nevertheless, I see the project as a success. The ambition was always about platform, and our work dramatically simplified how future improvements can be made. Nearly 800 million Highlander comments have been posted to

date. Highlander, known publicly as WordPress.com Comments, is available for free for any WordPress blog as part of Jetpack.

- *Jetpack is one of the most popular WordPress plug-ins in history.* Since my departure, Team Social and others at Automattic have continued to add features, driving adoption. For many web developers, it's now the first plug-in they install for their clients. Mullenweg believes it's a key part of the future of WordPress and invests in it accordingly.
- *Andy Peatling, Hugo, Tim, John,* and nearly every other employee mentioned in this book are still at Automattic and doing well. Noël Jackson left the company in 2011 and is an independent web developer and musician.
- *Mike Adams led Team Social for over a year.* He recently chose to join a new team at the company to work on new projects, a good experiment for him for sure. He was, to my delight, succeeded in March 2013 by Beau Lebens as the third lead of Team Social. Andy Peatling became the leader of Team Titan, working on the reader project to simplify how reading blogs are done. Tim Moore currently leads the newly formed Jetpack team.
- *Automattic has 170 employees* as of May 2013. The company continues to grow as does WordPress itself. Two new blogs are started on WordPress.com every second. The most recent statistics about WordPress are publicly available here: http://en.wordpress.com/stats/. Every month nearly 400 million people visit WordPress.com to read nearly 40 million new blog posts. Go to http://www.wordpress.com to start one.
- *Automattic was forced to leave their headquarters in 2011,* as the entire Pier 38 building was closed by the city of San Francisco for safety reasons. They designed a new office space that opened in May 2013 on Hawthorne Street, complete with an Automattic-branded shuffleboard table. http://www.wpdaily.co /automattic-office-san-fran/.

NOTES

Chapter Two

1. These are famous Microsoft interview questions from the 1990s. With a good interviewer, open questions (there is no right answer) let candidates demonstrate their problem-solving abilities. With a bad interviewer, which most are, these questions are torture devices.

Chapter Three

1. Caturday is a reference to the LOLCats meme, the popular images of cats doing cute things. All of the internal tools at Automattic referred to Saturday as Caturday. http://knowyourmeme.com/memes/caturday.

Chapter Four

1. "The Blogging Software Dilemma," December 26, 2003, http://ma.tt/2003/01/the-blogging-software-dilemma/.
2. Scott Berkun, "Microsoft No More," September 23, 2003. http://scottberkun.com/2003/microsoft-no-more/.
3. WordPress aided the writing career that has led to this book. More so, one reason for taking the job at Automattic was a chance to work on a product I used. It's rare in a career to use your expertise to contribute to something you use every day.
4. As Karl Fogel wrote in *Producing Open Source Software* (Sebastopol, CA: O'Reilly Media, 2005), "People should feel that their connection to a project, and influence over it, is . . . proportional to their contributions."

5.   Bob Sutton, *The No-Asshole Rule: Building a Civilized Workplace and Surviving One That Isn't* (New York: Business Plus, 2007).

6.   In May 2013, Automattic announced a secondary financing transaction of $50 million: http://ma.tt/2013/05/automattic-secondary/.

Chapter Five

1.   "How P2 Changed Automattic," May 5, 2009, http://ma.tt/2009/05/how-p2-changed-automattic/.

Chapter Six

1.   Mullenweg and others had some familiarity with Amazon.com's process known as Working Backwards, described by CTO Werner Vogels in 2006; http://www.allthingsdistributed.com/2006/11/working_backwards.html. It likely influenced how they worked, but I rarely heard it referred to directly, nor was the "process" Automattic used documented anywhere until now.

Chapter Seven

1.   A good overview of the history of fire teams is at http://en.wikipedia.org/wiki/Fireteam.

2.   David McCullough, *The Great Bridge* (New York: Simon & Schuster, 1983), 381.

Chapter Eight

1.   For the quote, famous in geek circles, go to "The Science in Science Fiction," *Talk of the Nation*, November 30, 1999, http://www.npr.org/templates/story/story.php?storyId=1067220.

2.   A. J. Jacobs, *The Year of Living Biblically* (New York: Simon & Schuster, 2007).

3.   The full list of commandments in the Old Testament can be found at http://en.wikipedia.org/wiki/613_commandments.

4.   Jody Thompson and Cari Ressler proposed a concept called ROWE, or Results Only Work Environment, at Best Buy, and they consult with companies on the concept (see http://en.wikipedia.org/wiki/ROWE). However, ROWE was never mentioned once at Automattic.

5.   See Alex Williams, "Working Alone, Together," *New York Times*, May 3, 2013, http://www.nytimes.com/2013/05/05/fashion/solo-workers-bond-at-shared-workspaces.html?_r=0 for background. For a directory of spaces

around the world, see http://wiki.coworking.com/w/page/29303049
/Directory.

6. Tracy Kidder, *The Soul of a New Machine* (New York: Back Bay Books, 2000), 63.

7. *Valve Handbook for New Employees* (Bellevue, WA: Valve Corporation, 2012), http://www.valvesoftware.com/company/Valve_Handbook _LowRes.pdf.

8. Franz Kafka, *The Trial* (New York: Oxford University Press, 2000).

Chapter Ten

1. Jane Jacobs, *The Death and Life of Great American Cities* (New York: Vintage, 1992; originally published 1961). The theory was developed by James Q. Wilson and George L. Kelling, "Broken Windows," *Atlantic Monthly* (March 1982).

2. Just as a broken leg will take more time to fix than a scratch, a simple incoming-versus-fix chart discounts possibly important details such as the scope of each issue.

3. A good summary of the problems with evaluating programming work based on lines of code is at http://en.wikipedia.org/wiki/Source_lines_of_code# Disadvantages.

Chapter Eleven

1. Eric Raymond, *The Cathedral and the Bazaar* (N.p.: Snowball Publishing, 2010).

2. Toni Schneider, "In Praise of Continuous Deployment: The WordPress .com Story," May 19, 2010, http://toni.org/2010/05/19/in-praise-of -continuous-deployment-the-wordpress-com-story/.

3. The best book documenting 1990s-era Microsoft software engineering practices is Michael Cusumano, *Microsoft Secrets: How the World's Most Powerful Software Company Creates Technology, Shapes Markets and Manages People* (New York: Free Press, 1998).

4. Mike Adams built a feature called Publicize, which automatically updated users' Twitter and Facebook accounts every time they published a blog post. But helping users understand its value and how to configure it were not simple.

Chapter Twelve

1. The Smile of the Child website is http://www.hamogelo.gr/.

Chapter Thirteen

1. Evan Hadingham, "Unlocking Mysteries of the Parthenon," *Smithsonian* (February 2008), http://www.smithsonianmag.com/history-archaeology /Unlocking-Mysteries-of-the-Parthenon.html.

Chapter Fourteen

1. Matt Mullenweg, "The Way I Work, Annotated," June 19, 2009. http://ma.tt/2009/06/the-way-i-work-annotated/.

Chapter Fifteen

1. Mayer's policy on remote work is discussed here: http://gigaom.com /2013/02/25/why-marissa-mayers-ban-on-remote-working-at-yahoo-could -backfire-badly/.
2. "Coralling the Yahoos," March 2, 2013, *Economist*, references a study conducted by Ipsos, a polling firm: http://www.economist.com/news /business/21572804-technology-allows-millions-people-work-home-big -tech-firm-trying-stop.
3. I have complied this list of fully distributed companies: http://scottberkun .com/2013/how-many-companies-are-100-distributed/.
4. From an interview with Tom Preston Warner at GitHub headquarters, October 2012.
5. Scott Berkun, "Would You Work from Home?" October 17, 2012. http://scottberkun.com/2012/poll-results-would-you-work-from-home/.

Chapter Sixteen

1. Jerry Hirschberg, *The Creative Priority: Driving Innovative Business in the Real World* (New York: HarperBusiness 1998).

Chapter Seventeen

1. "Manifesto for Agile Software Development," 2002, http://agilemanifesto .org/.

Chapter Nineteen

1. Scott Berkun, "Exceptions to Brooks' Law," January 11, 2006, http:// scottberkun.com/2006/exceptions-to-brooks-law/.
2. "Pinball Number Count Competition," August 8, 2003, http://www .youtube.com/watch?v=dnBAMQhtjEk.

3.   Matt Mullenweg, "Jetpack to the WP.com Cloud," March 9, 2011, http://jetpack.me/2011/03/09/blast-off/.

Chapter Twenty

1.   Michael Arrington, "Automattic Spurns $200 Million Acquisition Offer," October 29, 2007, http://techcrunch.com/2007/10/29/automattic-spurns -200-million-acquisition-offer/.

Chapter Twenty-One

1.   For an understanding of how emergent systems, like colonies or trade routes, work, read Steven Johnson, *Emergence* (New York: Scribner, 2002).
2.   For an overview of Parkinson's law of triviality see http://en.wikipedia .org/wiki/Parkinson's_law_of_triviality.
3.   It is possible to build a skyscraper one brick at a time, but there has to be a goal, plan, vision, or leader driving those incremental changes toward a big vision.
4.   "The Final Countdown" would become our deploy song—the music we played when about to launch a new feature.

Chapter Twenty-Four

1.   Richard Donkin, *The History of Work* (New York: Palgrave Macmillan, 2010).
2.   Matthew Crawford, *Shopcraft as Soulcraft* (New York: Penguin Books, 2009).

ANNOTATED BIBLIOGRAPHY

Most books about the making of important projects are told from the third person, typically with a journalist, and not a maker, holding the pen. Often it's clear they traded their sharpest words to get access to write about the project in the first place. Good, honest books about how things are made are hard to find. Over my career, I'd always wanted to see a book of this genre written by someone who had worked on projects of that kind themselves and could report honestly about what they experienced, as either an observer or a participant. When I realized I had a chance to write that book, I studied the journalistic forms of project reporting and first-person narrative.

Tracy Kidder's *Soul of a New Machine* (Back Bay Books, 2000) defined the tech project book genre, and it holds up best when you consider that the culture that Kidder captured from pre-PC computing is alive today in start-ups around the world.

I looked at first-person narratives by early employees at important companies: such as *Amazonia* (New Press, 2005) by James Marcus, *I'm Feeling Lucky* (Mariner Books, 2012) by Douglas Edwards, and *The Boy Kings* (Free Press, 2012) by Katherine Losse, but none told a primary tale of making, creation, and teamwork, themes I knew had to be central to *The Year Without Pants*. For a time, I expected this book to spend more time on open source philosophy, inspiring research on the origins of the movement. The film *Revolution OS* (http://www.revolution-os.com/) provided the best overview of the history. Karl Fogel's *Producing Open Source Software* (O'Reilly Media, 2005) was the best encapsulation of the project management view of what good open source projects do. Many habits I witnessed at Automattic are described procedurally in his book. Eric Raymond's *The Cathedral and the Bazaar* (O'Reilly Media, 2001) I'd read years ago, but reread since the contrast Raymond defined was central to my observations.

The greatest contribution to the form this book took came from reading first- and third-person accounts in other genres. I've always admired the work of journalist Ted Conover and reread his fantastic book *Newjack* (Vintage Books, 2001) about his year working as a prison guard. I reread George Orwell's *Down and Out in Paris and London* (Mariner Books, 1972), Anne Frank's *Diary of Young Girl* (Bantam Books, 1993), Henry Miller's *The Air Conditioned Nightmare* (New Directions, 1970), and dozens more. My goal was to internalize the advantages of first-person storytelling and avoid the downsides commonly found in memoirs. Tracy Kidder and his editor, Richard Todd, published *Good Prose: The Art of Nonfiction* (Random House, 2013), which was timed perfectly as nighttime reading while I worked on the second draft of this book.

I owe a debt of gratitude to the many writers whose work influenced this book.

ACKNOWLEDGMENTS

Thanks to Matt Mullenweg and Toni Schneider for granting permission for this project. Genoveva Llosa and Susan Williams deserve applause for their promethean confidence in a project that took big bets on narrative and convention-defying choices. Cheers to John Maas, Mary Garrett, and Bev Miller for making all the pieces come together. And a proud hat tip to cover designer Adrian Morgan for a spectacular act of provocative creation.

Deep thanks to Faisal Jawdat, Kav Latiolais, Richard Stoakley, Mike Adams, Beau Lebens, Andy Peatling, Matt Mullenweg, and Toni Schneider for honest feedback on early drafts. My gratitude to Andrew Nacin, Jason Cohen, Andrea Middleton, Noël Jackson, Paul Kim, and Tom Preston-Warner for letting me interview them about WordPress, Automattic, and remote work.

Cheers to all of the Automatticians I worked with who passionately pursue their ideals for great work.

To Tracy Kidder, Ted Conover, George Orwell, and Alain De Botton for inspiration.

Kudos to David Fugate, my agent, for various acts of magic and charming practicality.

Music listened to while writing this book: Audioslave, Cat Powers, Elizabeth and the Catapult, Joe Giant, The Kills, Tift Merrit, Beethoven, Mussorgsky, The Ramones, The Clash, The Pogues, Flogging Molly, Sera Cahoone, Johnny Cash, Hank Williams, Bruce Springsteen, Cake, Kaiser Cartel, White Stripes, Rollins Band, and Black Flag.

ABOUT THE AUTHOR

Scott Berkun is the author of four popular books: *Making Things Happen, The Myths of Innovation, Confessions of a Public Speaker,* and *Mindfire: Big Ideas for Curious Minds.* His work as a writer and speaker have appeared in the *Washington Post, New York Times, Wired Magazine, Economist, Fast Company,* and *Forbes Magazine,* and on CNBC, MSNBC, National Public Radio, and other media. His many popular essays and entertaining lectures can be found for free on his blog at www.scottberkun.com, and he tweets at @berkun.

INDEX

PHOTO CREDITS

Most photos in this book were taken by the author. All of the Automattic images, including screenshots of P2s and other tools, are used by permission.

Chapter 2: Berkun at work, by Jill Stutzman

Chapter 7: Automattic company photo, by Matt Mullenweg

Chapter 9: Automattic office at Pier 38, Beau Lebens (http://www.flickr.com/photos/borkazoid/3597020414 /sizes/o/)

Chapter 10: Diagram of how bugs are managed, conceived by Greg Brown.

Chapter 12: Photo of Andy Peatling, by Matt Mullenweg (http://ma.tt/2010/11/athens-with-social/)

Chapter 13: Team Social at the Parthenon, by Matt Mullenweg (http://ma.tt/2010/11/athens-with-social/)